A Pub Crawl Around
Essex

Graham Dover

A Pub Crawl Around Essex

Copyright © Graham Dover 2008
ISBN: 978-0-9558460-0-7
www.essexpubcrawl.co.uk

Printed and bound by Biddles Ltd, Norfolk

Published by: Colne Publishing
                  60 Colne Road
                  Halstead, UK
                  CO9 2HS
                  01787 478803
                  www.colnepublishing.co.uk

Introduction

This book is different from the usual pub guide that informs readers about the current price of beer in each pub, or details of what gastronomic delights the latest chef has available on his specials board. The management of pubs and their staff are always changing and such books can often be obsolete before they even reach the shelves in a book shop.

Instead, this book contains tales from the often-colourful history of some of the pubs in the county. There are also anecdotal stories, together with some romantic legend about events past. As part of my research, I visited each of these pubs and whilst there, it was of course necessary to try a pint or two in each of them.

Any pub that in my opinion did not merit a visit was immediately rejected, and as a result those that are included in this book can be recommended as a place to enjoy a nice pint, together perhaps with a pleasant meal, in friendly and convivial surroundings.

For those readers from the generation familiar with I-Spy books, there is a space at the bottom of each page to record the date of visiting each pub. Unfortunately, once you have completed your task, there is no congratulatory letter from Big Chief I-Spy to look forward to, but you are allowed to award yourself a small pat on the back.

I have enjoyed writing this, my first book, and hope that it gives its readers equal pleasure. On a personal note I would like to thank my partner, Lorraine for her splendid proof-reading.

I now start work on volume two.

Graham Dover

CONTENTS

5

Queens Head, Great Clacton

Originally built as a private house called Layes, the earliest records of this being an inn called the Queens Head date from around 1675. However, it was not until the Napoleonic era that the building came into its own. Large numbers of troops were stationed in the area, and the owner take advantage of the increased trade this brought to his business, by enlarging the premises. He also added the splendid full-length bow window at the front.

Some of these soldiers were from the Cameroon Highlanders, and it's said that the modest ladies of the village were shocked to see their bare knees in church.

At this time the upper floor was a ballroom, and whilst the enlisted men were drinking downstairs, the officers and their wives would be upstairs dancing minuets or waltzes, or perhaps the military two-step, to the strains of a small orchestra.

Beer sold on the premises was brewed next door in a row of cottages converted for the purpose, but when the Ipswich based brewer John Cobbold took over the pub, in 1844, brewing ceased here. The old brewery was then converted into a second pub, the Plough, and this is still in business just around the corner. The brewing company, Cobbolds, has now also disappeared, but there is on one exterior wall a fine tiled monument to its memory.

Around the year 1800, the Queens Head became the scene for the weekly corn market, and much trading was done by the local farmers. They used to meet to conduct their business every Tuesday until the practice discontinued about fifty years later.

At the same time it was the custom of this inn to have a selection of pipes on a table for anyone to use. There was also a tin of tobacco which could be opened by putting a halfpenny in the slot. However, anyone who failed to shut the lid afterwards was fined the sum of sixpence.

The nearby St John's church was not only the centre of religious life but also the home of local government. Sensibly though, the annual town meetings were held in the more amenable surroundings of the pub. After business had been completed the members sat down to a fine dinner, and the ensuing festivities continued at least late into the night, and often didn't cease until the following morning.

An inquest was held here in 1876 into the death of Mr. Henry Sadler, aged 34, who had been found in a nearby field with his throat cut. Mr. Manthorpe, a doctor who had been attending the deceased, said he believed that his patient had had a great deal of hard work of late and "his brain had evidently been overworked". The Coroner having summed up, the jury returned a verdict of suicide while in a state of temporary insanity.

16 St Johns Road, Great Clacton, CO15 4BS

Date visited

Swan, Braintree

This building extends a good way further back than is shown in the above photograph. It appears to have been built in three phases from 1550 to 1600, with the central section built first followed by the back part that has entry into the courtyard. Above the beam here, the date 1590 can be clearly seen. The front section was the last part to be completed.

The Swan is one of the oldest public houses in Braintree, being first formally recorded as an inn back in 1730. At the time some soldiers were billeted there. In 1762 it was known as the Black Swan and by 1823 it had changed colour and was called the White Swan.

The pub also appears in records of the civil court of the Lord of the manor when, during the 1850s, the landlord was charged with creating a nuisance by allowing a dunghill to accumulate in the street!

The original masonry and timberwork still remains, although at the turn of the twentieth century the timbers at the side were plastered over as a practical effort to help keep the warmth in. Thankfully this has now been removed.

The Swan is situated in one of Braintree's main shopping streets and it's strange to think that until 1938 there was a private, walled garden between the pub and the shops on the other side of the street. This was owned by Dr Jack Harrison who was quite a prominent person in the town. He also owned a large house nearby, and was in fact the first person in the town to own a motor car.

However, he did not make his fortune on the backs of the poor in the community as it was well known that he did not send bills to anyone that he did not think could afford to pay. It was rumoured though that he did make a bit on the side as a bookmaker.

He was also a noted practical joker and one day he sat watching a man dig a hole in the ground in order to erect a post, and then watched the man go into the Swan for some deserved refreshment. Immediately he called two boys over and paid them to fill the hole in again. "Be quick, before someone falls in" he called out.

When the man returned and couldn't find the hole, Doctor Harrison was seen having a good laugh at his window.

As recently as the 1980s, when opening hours were strictly limited, the Swan was granted a licence to stay open for longer on Wednesdays, which was market day in the town.

During the mid 1990s the pub extended into the adjacent premises which, although part of the original building, had until that time been a separate shop. With this increased size the Swan is now more able to handle its busy, all-day trade

22-24 Bank Buildings, Braintree, CM7 1UL

Date visited

Endeavour, Chelmsford

Originally built between 1808 and 1816, 'the house and buildings thereon' were left in the will of John Bodger to his wife Sophie, in 1818. However, she soon encountered financial problems and was forced to sell the property to cover the outstanding debts. The best price she could obtain was £280, and unfortunately for her, this failed to meet her obligations which were by then in excess of £500.

By 1844 the building consisted of separate tenements. In a directory of that year it was called a beershop for the first time and James Andrews was listed as a beer retailer. On the same premises James Timson was recorded as a plumber, painter and glazier.

In 1874, the Endeavour was sold into the Gray's brewery estate of public houses when they purchased the property for a price of £360. At this time George Thorndick was the tenant and he remained until about 1886 when Henry Wilsher took over.

During the following years there were several other changes of tenant until 1965 when Sidney Perry and his wife Edith took over. Edie, as she was affectionately known, continued on after her husband's death and was such a staunch supporter of the old tradition of brewing that when the Gray's brewery closed she held a state funeral for the last bottle. This was brought to the pub by taxi and solemnly buried in the back garden by one of the customers who was an undertaker. Anglia TV were there to record the ceremony as a slab was placed over the tomb bearing the words 'Underneath this stone lies the last of Gray's beer at the Endeavour 25th September 1974.'

The 'body' has now been exhumed and sits, pride of place, in a glass cabinet on one of the walls in the lounge bar.

In 1981 it was realised that the beer sold here was giving people more than just a hangover, when during that year twenty of the pub's regulars all became fathers. The cause was put down to Greene King IPA. Furthermore the landlady's grandson who helped in the pub 'suffered' the same fate and even the pub dog gave birth to a litter of seven puppies.

No one seems to know the origin of the pub's name, although it's thought it was named after the ship that carried Captain Cook on his first voyage across the Pacific Ocean. This ship is featured on the pub's sign, although now the picture on the other side is that of the American space shuttle of the same name.

Before the current building was erected, the local story is that there was previously a beer-shop here known as The Cage. The jail and hanging green were nearby, and it's said many felons were allowed to stop here for one last drink with their wardens. Hence the expression 'one for the road'.

351 Springfield Road, Chelmsford, CM2 6AW

Date visited	

Cock, Stock

The Cock stands right on the old border between the civil parishes of Stock and Buttsbury, and so became a convenient starting point for the annual 'beating the bounds' walk around the boundary. A detailed account of their perambulation on 21st April 1817 shows that it began by the window inside the tap-room of the Cock, and it was to the very same spot that the walkers later returned, presumably suitably thirsty.

There is a story that once, when a stranger died in the Cock, his body lay across the boundary line, and there was a disagreement about which parish should be responsible for his burial. After a heated discussion, it was eventually decided that the parish in which his head lay had to bear the cost. The ghost of this unknown visitor is still said to haunt the premises today.

The Cock has been much changed and enlarged over the years, and it's difficult to determine its exact age. However, some of the original parts are thought to date back to at least the 16th century.

The earliest reference to the Cock can be found in the 1527 will of John Ponder in which he bequeathed his feather bed to his daughter, Joan. He also left the alehouse to her and her husband, William Croxton, but unfortunately for them, there was a proviso that it had to be sold to pay his debts and funeral expenses.

In 1558, 'a common victualler' who was possibly the keeper of the Cock was charged with permitting people to play cards 'about the time of vespers on a feast day'. He was fined 3s 4d and warned that he faced six hours in the stocks, and possible banishment from the parish, as the consequences for any repeat offence.

Later that same century, Robert Newman who was landlord at the time, was one of thirteen local men who all received poison-pen letters informing them of their wives unfaithfulness. The letter purported to come from the curate of nearby Fryerning but he denied all knowledge of it. Eventually the case went to libel court, and it seems the culprit was Thomas Petchey who was an innkeeper at another house, and had some old scores to settle.

The same Robert Newman was involved in a court case in 1576, when the widow Agnes Sawen was accused at Quarter Sessions of being a witch. He was one of the accusers that she did 'bewitch and enchant' one Christopher Veale, so that he had become lame in both legs and was wasting away. She pleaded not guilty.

During the mid 1600s, George Weile, licensee of the Cock, issued tradesman's tokens because of the shortage of small coinage. These bore the image of a cock on one side with the inscription 'At the Cock in Stock' and his initials GAW on the other. Although they could only be exchanged at the premises of the issuers, such tokens were treated as part of the general currency until they were made illegal in 1672, following the issue of halfpennies and farthings by the Royal Mint.

Until the early 1960s, there was an open field on the site of the current car park, and to the delight of the local children, a funfair was regularly held there.

High Street, Stock CM4 9BJ

Date visited

George and Dragon, Mountnessing

In October 1774, there was a dramatic arrest at The George and Dragon, when on one Wednesday afternoon, two carriage-loads of customs officers and their assistants descended on the pub. They were looking for a gang of smugglers who had been observed frequenting the premises. Before they could arrest them, there was some gunfire which resulted in one officer being slightly wounded in the head, and one of the smugglers shot in the leg. The ball remained lodged in his ankle.

During the 1930s the landlord here was Jim Anderson, and he came up with some novel schemes to take the business forward. One of his ideas was to introduce the new sport of motor cycle scrambling in the fields at the rear of the pub. Today, such noisy events would not go down too well with local residents, but in those days there was an air of novelty about it and nobody seemed to mind having the peace of their Sunday afternoons disturbed. Eventually six old open-top buses were purchased and these were used as grandstands. Admission to watch the racing was sixpence, with an additional charge of three pence to gain entrance to the 'stands'.

294 Roman Road, Mountnessing, CM15 0TZ

Date visited	

Swan, Maldon

The 'Swanne' was first mentioned as an inn in an indenture dated 17th October 1737, when William Clarke and his wife Elizabeth were the owners. Later the same year they sold it to Philip Wood for £120. The price he paid included the inn, a large stable-yard to take a coach and four horses, a long range of stables and for good measure also an orchard at the back.

By 1803, Sam Askew worked here in the stables, but unfortunately he was killed by a blow from one of the horses in his care on October 14th.

In 1845 it cost Alfred Busbridge £987 to become the next owner, but in his case it certainly wasn't a long-term investment. He sold it, presumably for a profit, just four days later to the Chelmsford brewers, Wells and Perry. They in turn sold it to Gray and Son, the present owners, in 1906.

73 High Street, Maldon, CM9 5EP

Date visited

White Lion, Fobbing

The village of Fobbing is forever associated with the Peasants Uprising of 1381 which culminated in the villagers marching on London to meet with King Richard II. After initially agreeing to their demands, he subsequently reneged on his word, and many of the peasant leaders were later arrested and executed.

600 years later, they were commemorated by a plaque that was affixed to one of the walls outside this pub. The additional few lines of poetry, although appropriate, were actually written nearly 500 years after the event by the American poet, Ralph Waldo Emerson.

This building mainly dates from the fifteenth century, and it's thought this is the property that received justice's approval to sell alcohol in 1605.

Certainly it was established by the late 1740s, when the landlord at the time, the aptly named Richard Philpot, was paid thirty shillings to provide refreshments to the workmen who were carrying out improvements to the nearby church.

By 1821 William Rust was the landlord, and at the same time his wife Sara ran the village store from the same building. During some

16

renovation work in 1960, a handwritten note was found in the cellar in which Sara wrote that her husband had been responsible for a partition that had been erected there. She further mentioned that, as well as a fine carpenter, he was also a skilled undertaker.

In 1834, a wedding banquet was held at the White Lion following the marriage of William Rust's sister, Elizabeth, to William Bogue. However, during the course of the evening not everything went exactly to plan.

The problem arose because one of the villagers, a chap named Labor, still held a deep interest in Elizabeth, with whom there had been an earlier association. Perhaps fuelled by alcohol, this saga of thwarted desires descended into fisticuffs, and at some stage during the evening the unfortunate Mr Labor was held in front of the blazing fire to receive a most painful roasting.

He also suffered a bloody nose for his troubles, and subsequently the bridegroom ended up in court where he was fined the sum of one shilling, plus costs.

William Bogue eventually took over the running of the pub assisted by his wife Elizabeth, although the now-widowed Sara continued to live on the premises. In fact, when Bogue eventually made his inevitable journey to the great brewery in the sky, the two women settled down to run the pub between them.

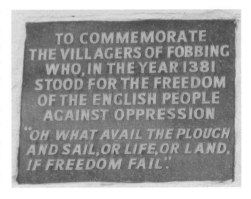

TO COMMEMORATE THE VILLAGERS OF FOBBING WHO, IN THE YEAR 1381 STOOD FOR THE FREEDOM OF THE ENGLISH PEOPLE AGAINST OPPRESSION

"OH WHAT AVAIL THE PLOUGH AND SAIL, OR LIFE, OR LAND, IF FREEDOM FAIL".

Legend has it that the White Lion is haunted by the ghost of an 18th century landlord's daughter, who was killed by him in a fit of rage. Known as the White Lady, she has been said to appear in the bar area and also upstairs in the bedrooms.

Lion Hill, Fobbing, Stanford-le-Hope, SS1 9JR

Date visited

17

Bell, Horndon-on-the Hill

Originally built in the 15th century, the first written mention of this building was in 1504 when John Abraham left to his wife in a will 'A house called the Belle'.

Fifty years later it was to witness the burning at the stake of local landowner, Thomas Higbed, after he fell foul of Mary Tudor's determination to reintroduce Catholicism. He was executed for failing to embrace this religion, and it's reputed that his wife was forced to watch the foul deed.

Moving forward several centuries to the days of horse-drawn coaches, a coach stopped here six days a week to pick-up and set-down passengers riding to and from Whitechapel. A balcony ran above the archway of the entrance, and suitcases were transferred there, directly from the stagecoach roof, to save the porters the effort of having to carry them up and down too many stairs.

It's possible that one of these passengers lost their wedding ring during this time as an old gold band, dug from the garden in the early 1900s, had the inscription 'As God decreed, so we agreed'. One can only speculate on the anxiety this loss may have caused somebody.

On Good Friday 1903, Jack Turnell took over as landlord of the Bell, and to celebrate hung a hot cross bun from one of the beams. He repeated this deed each following year and gradually this became a tradition that even today all successive landlords have continued.

During times of war when food was scarce, an imitation bun, sometimes made of concrete, was hung instead. Nowadays the oldest person available has the honour, each Easter, of hanging that year's bun.

In 1912, the local paper informed its readers that the current world flyweight champion, Mr Sid Smith, was currently staying at the Bell. He had won this title in a twenty-round match the previous year, and in fact had the honour of being the first ever holder of this title.

Before entering the pub, it's worth having a quick look at the sign hanging outside. This shows a single bell with the Latin legend 'Vivo Voco, Mortuos Plango, Fulgura Frango'. As all studiers of Latin, and customers of this pub, will tell you, this translates to 'I call the living, I toll for the dead, I shatter the lightning'. This saying summarises the different uses for church bells, and dates back to medieval times, when people generally believed in the power of bell-ringing to disperse thunderstorms.

In 1954, the Bell reached its 400th anniversary as a licensed house, and as part of the celebrations, a garland of Laurel was hung outside in a revival of the medieval practice, to signify achievement and honour.

High Road, Horndon-on-the-Hill, SS17 8LD

Date visited	

Sun, Feering

Thought to have been built around the year 1525, the earliest surviving deeds for this property are dated 1616, when it was owned by Robert Aylet, a lawyer working for the Archbishop of Canterbury. At this time the dining room looked completely different from its appearance today.

It contained magnificent oak panelling and 16th century carvings, which completely covered the walls. These carvings included the Royal Arms of England, together with the initials E.R. on each side, which suggest that Queen Elizabeth may have stayed here, in what was then a private residence, during her visit to Essex in 1579.

By the middle of the 19th century the Sun had declined from its former glory being described by one writer, who visited in 1845 to view the

20

carvings, as 'merely a beer shop'. A few years later another visitor commented on the money lavished on the building in the 16th century and wrote 'it is now an ale-house, and not even of a first rate class.' He then turned his attention to the customers with the comment that 'few but the poorest class of labourers sit in the parlour, and its beauty is unappreciated'.

Subsequently, this wood panelling was sold to a Mr Wooley, and was transferred to his private residence in Notting Hill. However, he did not enjoy it for long because in the following year a disastrous fire destroyed his house and all its contents.

During 1862, things looked up for a while after William Finch moved in with his wife and eleven children. In September of that year he obtained a full licence at the Witham Petty Sessions, and the Sun then officially became an inn rather that a beer-house.

By 1993, the pub was boarded up and once again in decline, until a new landlord and his wife took over, and immediately embarked on a program of improvements. They really should have had the support of the local council, but unfortunately these faceless bureaucrats saw it as nothing more than an opportunity to rake in some more cash, and issued a rate demand that was almost treble the previous year's charge.

However, this landlord was from Malta, the country awarded the George Cross during World War Two for its heroic struggle against enemy attack, and he demonstrated some of the same courage. He started boarding the pub up again, at the rate of one window a week, and said that when it was fully boarded he would return home and they would get nothing. After a few weeks of bad publicity in the local paper, surprise surprise, the council backed down.

3 Feering Hill, Feering, CO5 9NH

Date visited

Swan, Thaxted

The Bohun family owned a share of the manor of Thaxted during the 14th century, and this house took its name from their family crest which included a white swan. The inn has been called by that name at various times.

The earliest reference to the Swan as an inn dates back to 1539, when the owner was recorded as William Spylman. He sold more than just beer on the premises, and records from a few years later show that he supplied no less than four gallons of wine to the church situated opposite, to help them celebrate the Easter communion. He died the following year.

Some time later, the building passed through the hands of William Bullock, who on his death then left it to his grandson, Edward George. Mr George was a prosperous man, owning several houses and bits of land, but evidently he still felt a need to own a little more. In 1668, he was summoned to Dunmow court to answer a charge of taking a piece of the churchyard and 'laying it to his own ground'.

Following his death in 1618, Edward, who had inherited from his grandfather, in turn also missed a generation, and left the property, not to his son, but to his grandchildren. This may have been because his son, who shared the same name, had no interest in the business, and instead chose to make his living as a ship's carpenter.

By Georgian times, the Swan belonged to Harry Webb, who as well as running the inn was also a butcher. During his time as landlord, or perhaps just before, the front was rebuilt, hiding the gables that now can only be seen from the back of the building. For him it was a case of 'like father, like son' and he was later followed by his son in both professions

At one stage in its history the building was converted to three or four separate cottages, and parts of the partitions still remain today, together with the separate entrances.

For many years a livestock market was held in the yard of the Swan. A photo from 1910 shows pens of cattle and poultry for sale. Long after the market had discontinued, the old market bell still hung from the eaves at the rear of the building, but unfortunately this has now disappeared.

Beneath this yard were spacious cellars, and a deep well from where water was drawn for use in the maltings and brew-house that stood on the corner of what is now Margaret Street. These date from the time when the landlord brewed his own beer on the premises.

During 2006, the Swan closed for a major refurbishment, and when it reopened in December of that year, there was a new bar and impressive new look. £300,000 well spent.

Bull Ring, Thaxted, CM6 2PL

Date visited

White Horse, Sible Hedingham

Frederick Clarke and his wife, Sarah, took over the White Horse around the year 1873, and ran it as both an inn and also as a butchers. What is now the public bar was a separate shop at the turn of the last century.

Before that, it also served as the local courthouse, and perhaps it's the ghost of someone convicted at that time who has since been known to haunt the pub.

One previous tenant occasionally heard footsteps loud enough to send her upstairs looking for an intruder, but when she ventured upstairs no one was ever found. There was also the mystery of the front door bell. This was of the old type that needed the knob on the door to be tugged for the bell to ring in the backroom. One day, whilst it was snowing, the landlady saw and heard the bell moving, but after going to the door she could see nobody there, nor were there any footprints in the snow!

41 Church Street, Sible Hedingham, Halstead, CO9 3NT

Date visited	

Travellers Friend, Woodford Green

The Travellers Friend was converted from two private houses sometime in the 1830's, and since then has steadfastly refused to be influenced by the march of time going on all around it.

One unusual feature is the 'snob screens' that are sited at one end of the bar. These are a number of opaque, glass screens, each about 12 inches square, that rotate to form a barrier for the benefit of any customers who wish to discuss anything important, without being overheard or having their lips read

In 1924, Winston Churchill became the MP for Woodford, and by a strange quirk of fate, this was the same year that another campaigner, from the other end of the political spectrum, was opening a teashop just down the road from this pub. This was Sylvia Pankhurst, suffragette and co-founder of the British communist party, but it's unlikely that she would have welcomed him in for a cup of tea and a jam scone.

496/498 High Road, Woodford Green, IG8 0PN

Date visited

25

Anchor, South Benfleet

The framework of this building has been dated to sometime around 1381, and it was possibly built as a replacement for the local manor hall that had been burnt down during the peasant's revolt of that year. It was used as a court house, and additionally pilgrims often stayed here on their way to Canterbury when visiting the shrine of St Thomas a Becket.

Subsequently it was converted into an inn, and was listed in the 1770 Register of Ale-Houses. At this time though, it was known as the Blue Anchor.

In 1834, members of the vestry decided that it was time that the boundaries of the parish were formerly marked out and they met to 'put down posts at the proper points.' Their work done, they promptly adjourned to the Anchor for a well-deserved dinner.

By the 1920s, Sidney Lawrence had taken over a part of the building to run the village Post Office. His daughter Jane helped him and subsequently took over the business after his death. Later another daughter joined her, and opened a lending library on the premises. The good folk of Benfleet could borrow a book for a weekly charge of two pence.

After the First World War, the council dithered about where to site the proposed war memorial. Edward Land, landlord at the time, wrote to the council with the offer that, if sited outside his pub, he would finance the cost of illuminating it by gaslight 'at all such times as shall be deemed necessary.' However he did limit his potential expenditure to one shilling per annum.

This same landlord, whose father had run the pub for thirty years before him, was also involved when the town's first fire service was formed in 1924. The Buick tender was stored in the Anchor's stables, and as a reward Mr Land was allowed to ring the bell 'til he was red in the face' as the team of volunteers rode to the latest emergency.

The same indecisive council also spent over twenty years discussing about whether to introduce street lighting, but could never agree what action to take. It was eventually installed in 1926, although prior to that the Anchor had been the first building in the town to be lit by gaslight.

At the same time, the Benfleet Horticultural society was formed and held their first show in a marquee in the pub's garden. A local orchestra, and also the Shoeburyness Railway Silver Band, were on hand to provide the musical entertainment.

In 1973, whilst digging a trench at the rear, the skeleton of a man, minus his hands and feet, was found. He was most likely a criminal who had been executed and as a result could not be buried in consecrated ground.

During renovations in 1989, some of the original plaster was removed from one of the interior walls, and a child's tiny fingerprints were found. These were possibly 600 years old.

1 Essex Way, South Benfleet, SS7 1LS

Date visited

Bell, Wendens Ambo

This timber-framed building dates from the early 17th century and has, most likely, always been used as an inn. Certainly it was by 1767, when Arthur Newman was listed here as an inn-holder. This was an early example of a tied-house because at the time the building belonged to the Stortford Brewery.

A notice on the outside of the pub informs visitors about the unusual name of this village, and where it originates from. Until 1662, there were two separate villages next door to each other, one called Wenden Parva and the other Wenden Magna. Both had old churches that they could scarcely afford to maintain, and so the Archbishop of Canterbury gave his approval to the creation of a new parish called Wendens

Ambo. The choice of this name was quite straightforward as Ambo means 'both' in Latin.

In the summer of 1981, a re-enactment of a civil war battle was held in the village for a couple of days over one weekend. Not unnaturally, at the close of the first day the Bell was full of roundheads and cavaliers sharing a drink together. A strange scene for any time-travellers who happened to be there at the time.

The following year some major changes were made to the bell, when the dividing wall between the two very small bars was removed to form a single, more spacious area. At the same time the splendid inglenook fireplace was discovered, hidden away behind various later replacements.

It's possible that this work disturbed more than just some brickwork, because when new tenants moved in a couple of years later, they heard footsteps walking across the upstairs floor and back again. At the time there was no one else in the building.

Some locals think these sounds were made by the ghost of Mrs Goddard, who moved into this pub with her husband, William, in the early 1900s. She was always happy at the Bell, but following the death of her husband, reluctantly moved in with one of her sons, also called William, who by then had taken over the licence of another pub in the village, the Neville Arms.

Distraught by her loss, she died shortly afterwards and now her spirit is said to have returned to the place where she was the happiest. She never really wanted to move away.

Royston Road, Wendens Ambo, CB11 4JY

Date visited

White Hart Inn, Halstead

The White Hart is one of Halstead's oldest coaching inns, dating back to the 15th or 16th century. From here a regular coach service ran to Great Yarmouth, sometimes with four horses and sometimes with six. It's said that these coaches created quite an excitement when changing horses and picking up passengers, and they were awaited with great interest by the townspeople. A mail-coach also left every day at 7am for Kelvedon, carrying letters for onward transportation to London.

However, the days of coaching were numbered, and in 1914 a Mr Harrington placed an advertisement in the local paper where he 'begged to inform the public that he had purchased a large omnibus' and would be running a service three times a week from the White Hart, Halstead to the Orange Tree in Braintree.

St Bartholomew's day, 24 August 1662, was the last day for the nation's clergy to comply with the Act of Uniformity. Across the country over 2000 vicars and rectors refused to agree with this, and so were ejected from the church. The vicar of nearby St Andrews, William

Sparrow, was one of these, and he joined with like-minded people to form one of the country's first non-conformist churches. Their meetings were held in a barn at the rear of the White Hart until their own congregation hall was built in 1679.

By 1845, William Moye was the landlord, a position he was to keep for about 40 years. In addition to being a brewer and wine merchant, he also found time to supplement his income with some other activities. For a while there was an Inland Revenue office on the premises and later he became an agent for the Royal Farmers' Fire, Life and Hailstorm Insurance Company.

Opposite the White Hart is the fountain donated by George Courtauld, benefactor of the town, on the occasion of the golden jubilee of Queen Victoria in 1887. Subsequently, the good people of Halstead would assemble here for any good reason, and did so on 9th August 1902 to celebrate the coronation of King Edward VII. Dressed in their Sunday best, with the ladies in their splendid hats, all was going fine until the 21-gun royal salute was fired; the noise was so great that the pub windows were shattered.

At this time there was another pub, the Three Crowns, immediately next to the White Hart. This closed to become a garage in 1907, and the only evidence that now remains of its existence are the pub signs carved in the plasterwork on the upper floor. The owner of the garage, Harry Cooper, was an enthusiastic motorist, and often in trouble for speeding. In that year he was caught by PC Highwood travelling at a speed of 15mph and fined £5. He was, the constable said, travelling at 'a terrible pace'.

During the Second World War, the landlady herself, Eleanor Gray, appeared before magistrates charged with not adhering to the night-time blackout. She was caught by Police Constable Cole who stated that he had seen a bright light showing from a large, un-curtained window of the White Hart Hotel. Although the defendant pleaded not guilty, the chairman said that the showing of these lights had placed the whole town in danger.

15 High Street, Halstead, CO9 2AA

Date visited

31

Yew Tree, Great Horkesley

The Yew Tree, which sits on the old Roman road between Colchester and Sudbury, started life about 400 years as a pair of cottages, built from the timbers of old Dutch ships. It was first recorded as an alehouse in the 1870s although history is a little sketchy about the actual date of this transformation.

It is known that the annual village fair used to be held on the forecourt of this pub, and also it was a regular stopping over place for cattle farmers and their stock, on the way from Colchester market. Over 100 animals could be held in the paddock where the car park now stands. The farmers parked their carts, and stabled their horses at the rear, and then went to the bar where every man had a specially reserved nail on which to hang his harness.

On first impressions, it has everything you would expect from an old English pub, with a thatched roof, rustic timbers and open coal fires; however all is not as it seems.

In fact, during the summer of 1972, whilst some rebuilding was being carried out, a major fire broke out and swept through the building. Within minutes, the original thatched roof, and much of the upper half of the pub had been completely destroyed.

At this stage the owners could have thrown the towel in, but instead of this they rose to the challenge, and started a rebuilding program. The tavern's old frontage, complete with weatherboarding, was faithfully restored, and with a new thatch roof of Norfolk reeds it reopened in 1974.

At the time of this rebuilding, one local resident remembered back to the early 1920s, when as a seven year old child she had gone to this pub on an errand, and accidentally dropped her mothers gold watch, which she shouldn't have had with her, between a gap in the floorboards.

She was too scared to tell anybody about this accident, and so the watch remained in the same spot for over fifty years, until she went back for a look amongst the ruins, and retrieved it from the same place where she had dropped it.

Since this rebuilding, further improvements have been made at various times, and during 2000 the pub again closed for a refurbishment. When it reopened, the same lady, by then a sprightly 85 year old, was invited back to pull the first pint.

One benefit of this later refurbishment is the increased capacity. The Yew Tree has built up a well-deserved reputation for serving consistently good food and it can get very busy at weekends. However, those in the know, and readers of this book, can go to the rear of the bar where a turn to the left finds one in a very comfortable, open-rafted extension.

The Causeway, Great Horkesley, Colchester, CO6 4EG

Date visited

Shoulder of Mutton, Fordham

The building now known as the Shoulder of Mutton was originally built as a private house around the year 1380. During the 17th century, the original central hall was completely removed, and replaced with the present section to provide additional accommodation on the upper floor. At the same time, the new fashion of a brick chimney was added, and the days of sitting in a smoky hall gradually became a distant, bad memory.

In 1875, the inhabitants of the small village of Fordham woke up one Saturday morning to hear the news that an elderly couple, Solomon and Susannah Johnson, had been violently murdered. They were further shocked to hear that the crime had been carried out by the couple's youngest son, Thomas.

Jubal Partridge, who later became landlord of the 'Mutton', was the man who apprehended the culprit. He earned himself a sore arm for his trouble after receiving a couple of whacks from the actual murder weapon.

Halstead Road, Fordham, CO6 3LL

Date visited

Bluebell Inn, Hempstead

This pub was formerly known as The Bell, and probably hadn't been open for too many years when the landlord was summoned to quarterly sessions, in 1598, for keeping a disorderly house.

The name of this miscreant is not recorded, but it is known that by 1705 the landlord was John Turpin. He lived there with his wife Maria, and it was in that year that she gave birth to their son, Richard.

Mr Turpin was not only a brewer and ale-house keeper, but village butcher as well, and when his son grew up he sent him to be apprenticed at a butchers shop in Whitechapel. However, young Turpin could never take to honest work and soon began cattle-rustling and poaching. This eventually led to highway robbery and in 1739, when John Turpin still ran The Bell, his son, Dick Turpin, was hanged at York for horse-stealing.

High Street, Hempstead, Saffron Walden, CB10 2PD

Date visited

Bell, Woodham Walter

According to local tradition, the Bell was built in 1563, the same year as the nearby church, and if correct this would date it to 25 years before the defeat of the Spanish Armada.

The main gable, which overhangs the road in two successive risings, is carried on a massive oak beam intricately carved with vine leaves and tendrils. The atmosphere inside is one of unspoilt antiquity

The earliest recording of the inn was in 1593, when the landlord, Humfrey Willett, appeared at Quarter Sessions charged with keeping a disorderly house. It was also alleged that he allowed dancing on Sundays during service time.

Records from 1665 show that a later owner was Henry Oughan, who after inheriting from his father, left it in turn to his widow, Frances. Subsequently Isaac Osborne purchased the property in 1682, and lived there for thirty years, playing a prominent part in village life.

By the mid eighteenth century, Widow Wynn was the licensee, and when reassessed for window tax, she took the not uncommon step of reducing her liability by having some of the windows blocked in. They remained hidden, and long forgotten, until the 1930s when workmen accidentally discovered one of the windows that had been blocked up in 1757.

The brewers who owned the property at the time, then decided to remove all the plaster from the outside walls, and as a result not only was the original woodwork exposed, but a further five windows were revealed.

The inn was on the market again in 1823, when it was described as a 'substantial and commodious house' with a tap-room, liquor and beer cellars, two parlours and a bake house with an oven to bake seven bushels.

During the 19th century, most of the licensees had sidelines, and in addition to baker, these jobs included shoemaker, cattle dealer and carpenter. Fred Green, who was landlord before, during and after the First World War, ran a taxi service in his pony and trap, taking passengers to and from Hatfield Peverel railway station.

One of the inn's most renowned customers was Edward Bright, who died at the early age of 26 weighing in excess of forty five stone. His overcoat was left on a hook, and one day bets were taken about how many men could be buttoned up inside it at the same time. The record stood at no less than seven.

The Bell is reputed to be haunted although the ghost is rarely seen. In the early 1990s, a new landlord at the time expressed his doubts about the truth of this, and a picture promptly fell off the wall. Apparently, he never queried it again.

The Street, Woodham Walter, Maldon, CM9 6RF

Date visited

Plough and Sail, Paglesham

Although the village of Paglesham is mainly noted for boatbuilding and its oyster industry, the remoteness of the area also made it an ideal spot for smugglers to operate. It's said that at one time virtually everybody in the village was involved, even the local magistrate.

One notorious smuggler was William Blyth, who in addition to his illegal activities, found time to keep the village shop, and also act as the churchwarden. It's said, he tore out pages from church registers to wrap up his goods.

He was also the local tough nut, earning the nickname of Hard Apple. One day, during a game of cricket, a bull which had been terrorising the neighbourhood charged onto the pitch. Everyone ran for safety except Blyth, who caught hold of the bull's tail and refused to let go. As the bull dragged him over hedges and ditches, he held on steadfastly, until eventually the poor creature collapsed and died of exhaustion.

By 1890, there were over 30 oyster smacks operating in the area, and after a hard days work the crews would meet at the Plough and Sail for some well-deserved relaxation. Those who still had any energy left would perhaps have a game of ninepin bowling in the pin shed at the back.

Among the social occasions held here, was Hector Pettitt's coming-of-age celebration in 1892. All the men who worked in the oyster business owned by his father, Zachary, were invited, and at 5pm they sat down to what was referred to at the time as a substantial repast. Afterwards, refreshments, cigars and tobacco were provided.

The evening included various toasts and speeches, and culminated with Hector being presented with a marble clock. After standing to sing the national anthem, the party terminated at 10pm.

The pub was also the local bakery, and after the bread had been baked in the oven, villagers could use it to cook their meat, pies or other cooking. For this they were charged 1 penny each.

During the 1920s, charabancs regularly stopped outside bringing day-trippers from London's east end to sample the oysters. They would order up to 2 dozen at a time and eat them with brown sauce. It was usual to wash them down with a few pints of Guinness.

Behind the pub there used to be a separate tearoom and it was here that Mrs Loader, landlady for over 30 years, used to serve her celebrated Paglesham pie. The ingredients for this included steak, kidney and not surprisingly, oysters.

East End, Paglesham, SS4 2EQ

Date visited

39

Three Horseshoes, Mole Hill Green

Parts of this building are thought to be 500 years old, although its early history has been lost in the mists of time. The earliest records that have been found are dated 1769, when Henry King was listed as the landlord. By 1800, Mary King, presumably his widow, ran the business to be followed by James King, presumably their son.

In the census of 1861, James Staines was listed as the tenant of the Three Horseshoes, and was described as a beer house keeper and farmer, with 40 acres of land, employing two men. In fact it remained a working farm until as recently as the 1930s.

The choice of the pub name would have indicated that there was a blacksmith or farrier not far away, and in this case it was part of the same set of buildings. Early records show that there was also a shoemaker and tailor on the premises. Incidentally, why three horseshoes and not four? Because the horse would stand on three whilst being shod.

The pub was owned by the Rush family until at least 1894, and then it briefly belonged to the Hawkes Brewery before being sold to Benskins in 1898. They continued to own it until 1967, when it was sold to Ind Coope for £7,300.

In June 1903, an inquest was held at the Three Horseshoes into the death of 13 year old George Stock, who worked for a local farmer, and had been run over by a cart a few days earlier. A witness said that the boy appeared to fall down, but could not be sure if the horse had knocked him over or whether he just tripped and fell. He further remarked that when calling the horse to stop it did so, but not before the wheel of the cart had passed over George's head and killed him. The jury returned a verdict of accidental death.

One likely visitor around this time was the future King Edward VII, when Prince of Wales. He passed by on a number of occasions, whilst staying at Easton Lodge, and given his liking for good ale would have found it difficult not to pop in and sample the local fare.

In the early part of the twentieth century, there was a fair held every year in the field behind the 'Shoes', with all the traditional attractions of roundabouts and swings etc. This was always one of the highlights of the village year, especially for the children, although the adults enjoyed themselves as well. The men in particular, were said to be very good shots on the coconut shies, although whether this was before or after a few pints of Benskins is not known.

In 1930, the tenancy was taken over by Jack Sergeant who was a former London policeman and weighed in at 22 stone. Unfortunately, he died just before Christmas after only five years service, but his widow, Florence and then his son, Philip continued to run the concern for another 25 years.

When BAA announced their plans for a second runway at Stansted Airport, it became apparent that part of the environmental cost would entail sending in the bulldozers to demolish this fine building. Cheap flights anyone?

Mole Hill Green, Takeley, CM22 6PQ

| Date visited | |

41

Black Lion, High Roding

High Roding is one of eight places in close vicinity that take the second part of their name from the river that runs near them all on its way to Barking Creek.

Among these are Abbess Roding which is so-called because it once belonged to the Abbess of Barking, and White Roding which was named from the appearance of its newly built church back in Norman days. Quite simply, High Roding is called thus because it is fifty feet higher than any of its neighbours.

The Black lion is a former coaching inn that has been traced as far back as 1397. It is believed to stand on the site of an earlier building and some of the wooden beams from that were used in this 'newer' construction.

The earliest official records, lodged at Chelmsford, are dated 1677 when this was listed as an inn with stagecoach facilities for the relay route to London. It stands on one of the many ancient roads built by the Romans, this one stretching from London onwards to Cambridge.

Another more recent link with Chelmsford is Ridley's brewery that was based in that town. They bought this inn in 1924 but, following the surrender of their independence in 2003, it now forms part of the Greene King empire.

During the mid 1970s, Ridleys received a letter from an American who had traced his family tree back to the Pilgrim Fathers and their voyage to the New World in 1620. The letter contained evidence that one of his ancestors had in fact kept the Black Lion on behalf of a wealthy landowner, and also looked after a number of livery horses for coaching purposes.

For many old pubs it is 'de rigueur' to have a ghost to boast about, especially to any visiting Americans looking for family history, and in this respect the Black Lion does not disappoint. Investigations by a former landlord uncovered details about the ghost of a Roundhead officer who apparently resides in the old hayloft, although whether the two of them ever came face to face is unknown.

There are two separate bars and a further restaurant area here, and between them there is everything one would hope to find in a fine old Essex pub. These include exposed wooden beams, block-wood floors, mellow brickwork, old oak tables and also a good collection of sporting memorabilia.

However, when one of the internal walls was removed some years ago something was found that was not expected. A number of gold coins had been hidden there, although who they originally belonged to remains a mystery.

The Street, High Roding, CM6 1NT

Date visited

Half Moon, Belchamp St Paul

The picturesque Half Moon, which dates from 1685, sits overlooking the village green in the village of Belchamp St Paul. During the early 1990s it featured in the BBC series Lovejoy when part of the 'Peking Gun' episode was filmed in the front garden.

On 26th April 1923, The Suffolk and Essex Free Press reported that a very enjoyable evening was spent at the Half Moon by a large number of people 'listening in' to a wireless concert. The paper also commented that, although the village has neither telephone nor telegraph, people are now able to hear the news. The broadcast that night came from London and Glasgow.

The 'luxury' of those radio broadcasts would not have been available to the villagers for too long after that, without the quick actions of the landlord at the time, William Russell. When fire broke out the following year it was him alone who put it out. The same newspaper, noting the straw roof, said that if the fire had not been discovered, the structure and the valuable wireless installation would have been destroyed.

Coles Green, Belchamp St Paul, CO10 7DP

Date visited

Wooden Fender, Ardleigh

The strange name for this pub originates from the time when there was a large pond in the field opposite, and a wooden fence had been erected around it to 'fend' off cattle and stop them falling in.

It was first recorded as a coaching house in 1625, when it stood on the London to Harwich route. An advert from 1763 boasted that the journey would take just a day and a half 'if God permit'. The fare was eight pence.

The inn was a welcoming site for travellers of the time as the forest around was once a notorious haunt for outlaws. However, whether it was really such a safe haven is not necessarily the case, because one of the landlords was in league with some of these rogues. He would tip them off about any guests worth robbing, and they would then wait round the corner for their next unsuspecting victim.

During the height of the witch trials in the mid 1600s, the Witch-Finder General, Matthew Hopkins, was known to have held a meeting in the taproom here.

Colchester Road, Ardleigh, CO7 7PA

Date visited

The Castle, Earls Colne

The oldest part of this building is the east cross-wing which dates back to around 1375. It started life as a private house called Olmsteads, and was owned by the local priest.

Whether built at the same time is not known, but rumour has it that there was once a secret tunnel which ran from here up to the church and then on to, what was at the time, the priory. It's said that later this was used as a hiding place by monks being persecuted during the reformation.

Perhaps one of the monks was discovered and met with an unpleasant end, and this may explain why the ghost of an old monk has been regularly seen by customers, especially in the garden. One local policeman, who saw him when he was a young child, still refused as an adult, to go anywhere near the garden after dark.

The old monk is not the only ghost who has made its home in this building; a girl in her early twenties has also been seen. Fleeting glimpses of her, wearing a blue dress, are often seen by the current landlady, but she has no fear of her as she is sure that the girl means no harm.

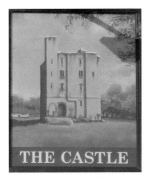

THE CASTLE

By the 1700s, the building was a meeting house for religious gatherings, possibly the Quakers, and at this time the Latin inscription, *sic transit gloria mundi* was painted above the fireplace. This translates to: 'so the glory of this world passes away' and is now read at the coronation of every new pope to remind him, that despite all the grandeur of his position, he is still a mortal man.

One wall in the afore-mentioned east wing is completely covered by a mural of what appears to be a medieval dinner, but do not be fooled into thinking this is as ancient as the 300 year old inscription above the fireplace.

In fact this dates from as recently as 1977, and the characters portrayed were regulars of the pub at the time. The only exception was the guv'nor who can be seen, sitting in the middle of the front row, and his wife who was portrayed as the serving wench.

At the time that this was painted, some of the older regulars could probably remember when the Castle first opened its doors to the drinking public. This was in the mid 1930s when, after it had stood empty for some time, Greene King bought the premises and converted it into a public house.

77 High Street, Earls Colne, CO6 2QZ

Date visited

47

Bull, Langley Lower Green.

The Bull was opened around the year 1780 by the Hawkes Brewery, who were based in the nearby town of Bishops Stortford. A favourite beer for tipplers at the time was their 'Hawkes Entire' bitter stout, which they advertised as a 'most nutritious ale'. Eventually, the estate of this company had increased to over 150 pubs when it was taken over by the larger Benskins brewery in 1898, for a cost of £270,000.

Traditionally, Langley was a place where drovers and graziers stopped with their cattle and sheep, on their way to the London markets. Whilst the animals were enjoying the fine pasture and water from the stream, their owners were inside here enjoying what would have been their preferred refreshment.

At this time the cottage opposite was used to house the local poor. A notice on its wall from the village constable warned them that 'beggars will be whipped'.

In 1870, and for the next twenty years, the landlord went by the name of George George. This possibly confused some of his unwary customers, especially after a few pints of Hawkes Entire. He was listed as a beer-seller and farmer, and lived on the premises with his wife, Emily and seven children.

The outside appearance of the Bull is little changed since those days. It still has the same narrow-paned lattice windows, which must be an inconvenience when it comes to cleaning, but they are listed and cannot be replaced.

During the 1980s, the village GP, who was based eight miles away, began to hold a weekly surgery every Wednesday afternoon in the Bull. This was a great idea for elderly patients and anyone without a car, but unfortunately did not meet with the approval of the NHS inspectors.

They had no objection to the surgery being held on licensed premises, and were not even worried if any patients took the opportunity for an out-of-hours tipple. However, they were concerned about the privacy of the patients, and so ordered the doctor to cancel this arrangement.

The Bull is home for, amongst others, the local football and cricket teams. The latter is taken very seriously in the village and the team has on occasions reached the finals of national cricket competitions. Fielding can be a dangerous occupation though, as a public road runs alongside the wicket and through the outfield.

Another, less energetic game, associated with this pub is 'Penny in the Hole' which is played by pitching pennies across the room and into a hole carved into the bench seat by the bar. This is a traditional East-Anglian pub game, and a supply of the old pre-decimal coins is available behind the bar for anyone who wants to try it.

The rules have been lost in time, so anyone playing the game has to make their own up as they go along. Generally, what happens is that the person who successfully throws the most coins is the winner, and the person throwing the least buys the beers. Pretty straight-forward then.

Langley Lower Green, Saffron Walden, CB11 4SB

Date visited

Angel, Kelvedon

The Angel seems to have earned a reputation over the years for not necessarily being the most proper of places. As far back as July 1596 it was recorded that 'a certain alehouse in Keldon called after the sign of the Angel, is maintained by Wymian Robinson, who doth use the same very disorderly.'

In 1632, George Browne and his wife were the subject of a Church Visitation for allowing company to drink beer during Divine Service. George, who was not at church due to a sore leg, pleaded in his defence that only one gallon had been drunk.

Things didn't seem to have improved two centuries later, when in 1854, Thomas Levericke appeared at Quarter Session Rolls charged with keeping great disorder in his house, and allowing cards, dice, tables and other unlawful games. It was also claimed that 'the said Thomas dothe make his horse bread too light.'

In 1809, the property was put up for sale by auction at Garraway's Coffee House in Cornhill, London. The freehold estate included 'nine airy sleeping rooms, four parlours and stabling for 30 horses.' The prospectus also said that 'it gave advantageous opportunity to a person wishing for a life where profit and respectability were united.'

During the Napoleonic wars, in September 1811, the Prince Regent with his brothers, the Dukes of York, Cumberland and Cambridge, stopped at the Angel after reviewing the troops stationed at Colchester. Whilst there, it was recorded that they were able to 'partake in an elegant cold collation, before setting off to London with fresh post horses'.

An earlier royal connection was that with King William III, who was a frequent visitor here on his journeys to and from Harwich. Specifically, the diary of a chap named Bufton records that on October 20th 1692, the king 'went through Kelvedon and stayed and dined at the Angel'.

In 1831, David Hume, former butler to the late Dr. Badley purchased the property and announced 'to the gentry and public in general that he had entered the above concern'. "The greatest care" he said "would be taken to render the lodging establishment comfortable".

During its heyday as one of the town's premier coaching inns, the corner of the road where the Angel stood was renowned as a tight spot to drive coaches around. One particular driver, Israel Alexandre, called it the "very devil" of a corner after nearly crashing whilst trying one particular manoeuvre.

The awkward corner remained a problem for drivers until 1939, when the original inn was demolished, and this replacement built in a safer position further back from the road.

St Marys Square, Kelvedon, CO5 9AN

Date visited

Whalebone, Fingringhoe

The earliest records of this grade II listed building go back to 1735, when it was mentioned in Court Rolls as being a former property of the church. At that time it was probably already known as an alehouse, although it was not until 1769 that it was first registered as the Whalebone Inn.

No one now is really sure where the name originated and among the locals there seem to be two main lines of thinking. For centuries a whaling industry existed in the North Sea and one theory is that the pub was named after that. For many years, a whole jawbone stood outside the pub but its origin is unknown, and another mystery is where it went to. Apparently it was sent away for restoration some years ago but was never returned. At one stage, a wooden substitute was put there but that too disappeared.

It's possible that the original jawbone could have been from a monstrous whale, said to be two hundred and forty feet long, that was killed near Colchester in 1677.

Another possibility about the name has nothing to do with those magnificent mammals from the deep. It could simply be a derived from the ancient Saxon word 'Walbon' or 'Valbon' which translates to welcome.

During the Napoleonic wars, those living near the east coast lived in constant fear of invasion. In April 1798, a meeting was held at the Whalebone to decide the most effective way to preserve property, and also annoy as much as possible 'our most inveterate enemies the French'. Plans were also made to drive all sheep and cattle to upland places.

When peace was declared from midnight of 13th October 1801, the landlord held a party that eventually lasted for three days. A whole ox, stuffed with potatoes, was roasted outside, and a drunken mob described as up to fifteen hundred people managed to get completely out of hand. At one stage they took food 'even off the plates of those gentlemen that were eating it'.

All the events of this celebration were recorded at the time by one Joseph Page, and he summed up the grand finale as follows. "A vast number of intoxicated men, with flags flying and firing of cannon, paraded about the parish, dragging the cannon with them." Just as well for the French that they didn't invade!

Another former landlord was a retired shipwright, and his love of the river prompted him to design a punt which was propelled by the driving gear of an old penny-farthing bicycle. The machine worked well and he was regularly seen 'cycling' along the River Colne en-route to Colchester.

The garden at the Whalebone, which overlooks a peaceful valley, is said to have some of the most scenic views in north-east Essex. Opposite is a pond with good fishing, and the nearby giant oak tree is reputed to be one of the largest in the county. Legend has it that this grew from an acorn placed in the mouth of a highwayman who was executed and buried on the spot some three centuries earlier.

Chapel Road, Fingringhoe, CO5 7BG

Date visited

Crown, Wormingford

During extensive renovations in 1982, when some old brickwork and plaster was removed from an upstairs room, two mummified cats were found, one each side of the fireplace.

It was customary among cottage and inn builders in the Middle Ages to bury a cat alive in the premises to provide psychic protection, and this dates the building to around 1600, when chimneys were still a new and untried invention.

Since the discovery, and removal, of the cats, some strange events have taken place at the Crown. The latch on the outer door has often been violently agitated, long after the inn has been closed for the night, and it is said that any new landlord when first taking over experiences a feeling of great chill as if someone, or something, is checking on him. This is only felt once in any tenancy.

Main Road, Wormingford, Colchester, CO6 3AB

Date visited	

Rainbow and Dove, Hastingwood

This pub was originally known as just the Rainbow, and the current name, with its biblical connotations, evolved because a bush in front of the pub was trimmed into the shape of a dove. The bush has long disappeared but there's still an old photo of it on one of the walls.

The building has had quite a chequered career. It started life as a farmhouse, and subsequently was recorded as a licensed tavern by the time of Oliver Cromwell. His New Model Army was stationed on the nearby common in 1645.

During the 1930s a local chap, Bill Butt, worked at the pub as a part-time gardener. He was unpaid and happy just to work for as much beer he could drink during his labours, but such was his drinking capacity that the guv'nor was forced to cancel the arrangement. It is not recorded how Mr Butt felt about this, but if he was disgruntled it might explain why the bush was cut down.

Hastingwood Road, Hastingwood, CM17 9JX

Date visited

The Nags Head, Moreton

On the outskirts of Ongar, somewhere to the north of the A414, stands the tiny village of Moreton, and anytime one is in the vicinity it is well worth making the detour here to savour the delights of the Nags Head.

Once inside there are plenty of the wooden beams and uprights you would expect from a sixteenth century building, and at one end a massive brick fireplace houses a welcoming coal fire in the winter months.

The pub actually started life as two separate houses and the split-level floor gives an indication to the position of the original dividing wall.

The Nags Head has always been known by this name except for a brief period in the mid 1980s. This was when it was taken over by the Massey family, who in an unbelievable display of ego renamed it the Moreton Massey. When they eventually moved on, probably to take

56

over the Trump Tower in New York, sanity prevailed and the new owners quickly reverted back to the original name.

There is a good selection of reasonably priced food on the menu and also a list of the changing specials shown on the blackboard. This can eaten at one of the informal tables scattered around the bar or in the separate restaurant area at the rear. During the summer it can be very pleasant to sit at one of the picnic tables in the garden.

The village of Moreton's claim to fame is that a few years ago it won a prize for the best kept village in Essex, and there is definitely a real rustic charm about the area. This particular pub was also in the limelight when Ian McShane turned up with his film crew to record a scene from Lovejoy. Strangely though there's no photographic record of this on display anywhere.

What there is on one wall however, is a reproduction of Charles Lees' famous painting 'The Golfers' which was commissioned to commemorate a famous golf match played at St Andrews in 1841. For those who are interested, the chap standing upright to the left of the hole is the aptly named Major Fairplay, and the painting is reputed to capture the exact point in time when his shot is on its way across the green and into the hole to win the match.

There are actually two fine pubs in this village, the other being the White Hart, and every Boxing Day teams from each compete at various games and obstacle races. The day ends in a tug-of-war across a nearby brook and as well as sacrificing bragging rights for a year, the losing team also ends up rather wet.

Church Road, Moreton, CM5 0LF

Date visited

Cross Keys, Saffron Walden

Saffron Walden gets its name from the Saffron crocus that was grown in the area during the Middle Ages. This was used for medicinal and culinary purposes, and also to make dyestuffs.

By 1647, at the height of the English civil war, it was in this town that Oliver Cromwell made his headquarters. He was based at the nearby Sun Inn, but here at the Cross Keys, well out of sight from their boss, roundheads were known to drink to the defeat of the royalist cavaliers.

At this time it was known as the Whalebone, although by 1709 it had changed its name to the Bull's Head. Title deeds show that when it changed hands in 1754, the name was changed yet again and it took over the name of the Cross Keys Inn from a nearby inn that was closing down.

It's thought that the building was constructed about 1450, and romantic legend has it that the corner post was still a living tree when the structure was built around it.

As with many old buildings, there is a ghost in this building, although very unusually he only appears once a year and this is always on Christmas Eve. Reminiscent of Jacob Marley in the Charles Dickens classic 'A Christmas Carol'.

Past landlords have reported this haunting and have all heard the same footsteps made by an invisible entity on the upper floor. These footsteps can be heard clearly from downstairs, and are said to be heavy enough to make the ceiling creak. Strangely, they walk along a passage which ends with a blank wall.

It has been suggested that it is the ghost of one of the roundhead soldiers who used to frequent this inn. It is the weight of his armour that makes the footsteps so heavy.

At some stage in the life of this pub, the outside was completely plastered over, and this wasn't removed until 1920. At the time some additional windows, previously blocked-up were discovered and reopened. It also became apparent that the top storey was not part of the original building but added on later, probably in the late 18th or early 19th century.

By the end of the twentieth century, the Cross Keys had considerably grown in size. From just being on the corner of the High Street, it expanded along King Street by taking over some of the shops which stood behind it and were in its way.

Perhaps some people, who as children purchased a bar of chocolate or a packet of wine gums in Barrett's or Molly's Candy Store, now go back to the same building, as adults, for something a little stronger.

32 High Street, Saffron Walden, CB10 1AX

Date visited

Woodman, Stanford Rivers

The oldest part of this building is said to date back to about 1070, and since then various other sections have been added. The main area has a large fireplace with the year 1674 carved into it, whilst the back part of the building is early 19th century.

Over the years, a large number of celebrities are said to have spent some time in the Woodman. These include a range of personalities from politicians such as Winston Churchill, Neil Kinnock and John Major, to singers such as Frank Sinatra, Madonna and various Beatles.

According to a potted history on the wall, there have also been a few more infamous visitors. These allegedly include an 18 year old student named Saddam Hussein, who was here back in the mid 1950s, and on another occasion Charlie Kray, brother of east-end gangsters Ronnie and Reg was a guest. Presumably they counted the cutlery after he left.

From earlier times, such names as Samuel Pepys and Daniel Defoe are known to have visited. The latter wrote of the 'wondrous retreat from hell, that lovely inn at Stanford ye Rivers, ye Woadman, has proofed to be'.

Dr Johnson is another man of words who stayed here, and he also found good things to say when he wrote about the 'courtliness and winsomeness of the wenches'. Whilst at the Woodman, he also purchased three pounds of sausages to take back to the coffee houses of the City of London.

The tradition of selling sausages here started back in medieval times, when a retired Norman soldier opened a shop in this very building. Despite living in an area populated by Saxons, he was apparently quite a popular chap, and so were some of the specialties of Norman food that he introduced. This included a delicacy that he called 'A la Sosseige' although his customers found it easier just to ask him for sausages.

On 22nd December 1906, the Woodman Slate Club, under the presidency of Mr J Judd, met here, and distributed just over a pound to each of its forty members. Afterwards, they sat down to supper whilst being entertained to a selection of music played by the Roding Valley Brass Band.

In 1999, Britain's oldest brewery, Shepherd Neame, acquired the Woodman, and added to their estate of over 350 tied houses. Within a few years it was given a trophy as their Pub of the Year, not to mention a nice winner's cheque for £1000 for the landlord. This was first time any pub from outside their home county of Kent had been given such an award.

London Road, Stanford Rivers, CM5 9QF

Date visited

White Hart, Manningtree

The original parts of the White Hart date from the early 16th century, with further additions made in the next couple of centuries. Samuel Pepys is believed to have stayed here in the 1660s, on his way to visiting the Royal Shipyard at Harwich.

The parish Easter Dinner was held here in 1771; there was a show of lambs and sheep in 1773, and in 1783 the delightfully named Society for Prosecuting Horse Thieves held its annual meeting on the premises.

In 1828, the local population were fascinated by what was to become known as The Red Barn Murder. Sometime in the previous year, Maria Marten had left her home for a clandestine meeting with her lover, William Corder, and her family never saw or heard from her again. One year later, her body was found buried in the barn where the lovers had arranged their secret rendezvous.

Eventually, Corder was arrested, and it was at that stage Nathanial Dale, landlord of the White Hart, realised that this was perhaps the same man who had recently stayed at his hotel and presented a forged cheque at the bank opposite. He told the bank manager of his suspicions and together they travelled to Colchester and identified the criminal.

62

Some of the stolen money was later recovered by the bank, although it made little difference to Corder. Following a short trial, he was found guilty and executed later the same year. His body was removed for dissection and the surgeon responsible, the rather macabre George Creed, later had an account of the man's trial bound in leather made from Corder's skin.

Nathanial Dale was to remain landlord here for nearly fifty years, and during that time he built a new carriage entrance, a billiard room, and a ballroom and bar.

In 1839, a stagecoach left here every day at 12 noon, en route to London, via Colchester and Chelmsford. An advertisement at the time stated that it returned every night at ten, but considering the speed that these coaches could reach, it's more likely that there were two such coaches, one travelling in each direction.

By 1859, the White Hart was advertised as a Family and Commercial Hotel, posting House and Inland Revenue Office. In 1882 James Hibbard was recorded as a victualler and Inland Revenue Officer.

Until the 1930s, beer was supplied here from Alston's brewery located on the immediate opposite side of the road. It's reputed that there was an underground tunnel running between the brewery and the pub, but no evidence has been found to prove that this is anything more than just rumour.

Yet another rumour is that the voice of Witch-finder General, Matthew Hopkins, can sometimes be heard in the building. He lived in the area for a while, and during the mid 1640s used this inn as the site for some of his grisly trials. However in 2004, when Living TV shipped in their Most Haunted Live team, the best they could come up with after three days investigation was that 'Something is eerie'.

9 High Street, Manningtree, CO11 1AG

Date visited	

Swan, Brentwood

This inn was originally called the Argent, and then its name was changed to the Gun. It wasn't until 1783 that it became known as the Swan. It is reputedly haunted by the ghost of William Hunter, who was held here for two days prior to his execution for Protestant beliefs in 1555.

Since then there have been continued stories of strange events and happenings. These include copper plates bearing religious inscriptions being hurled across the room, doors locking themselves, and papers being moved around. Domestic animals have occasionally acted strangely and the dog of one former landlord steadfastly refused to enter certain parts of the building.

If, indeed, it is the ghost of William Hunter who is responsible for these occurrences, he must know that he is not now 'living' in the same actual building in which he was incarcerated. This was demolished and replaced by the present structure in the middle of the 1930s.

123 High Street, Brentwood, CM14 4RX

Date visited

Crown, Elsenham

In December 1910, the Crown Hotel played host for the annual dinner of The Elsenham Sparrow Club. After the fine meal had been consumed, the secretary stood and reported to the membership that 2,946 heads of sparrows had been handed in during the year ending Michaelmas 1909. In its twenty years of existence, he said, the club had been responsible for the destruction of over 54,200 sparrows.

There used to be a row of trees along the front of the pub and during the 1930s, the notice board for the local cricket club was fixed to one of these. This was convenient for any players on their way into the pub to read if they had been selected to play the next weekend. A framed copy of their fixture list for 1934 can now be seen on the wall in the public bar.

One previous landlady claimed to have regularly seen the ghost of a lady in the restaurant area. She was not frightened and always said hello, but not surprisingly, never received any reply.

The Cross, Elsenham, CM22 6DG

Date visited	

Crooked Billet, Leigh-on-Sea

For some people, a plate of cockles or whelks is the perfect food to wash down with a few pints of good ale, and for those so inclined, there is no better place than the Crooked Billet in the old fishing village of Leigh-on-Sea.

On a summer evening, it can be very pleasant to sit on the terrace at the front and enjoy the panoramic views of the estuary, whilst enjoying a platter of your choice from the long-established Osborne's shellfish stall. The two businesses share the same seating area.

During the winter months, when it's too cold to sit outside, both of the separate bars are comfortable enough with their real fires. The bar to the left, which was the old public bar, can boast an inglenook fireplace which is probably as large as that in any pub in the county. It could easily pass as the prototype design for a bus shelter.

Around the walls are many old photos of the area, and it's not too difficult to look at these and conjure up in your mind the days when this pub was frequented by smugglers and fisherman of times past.

From a more recent era, a plaque on one wall commemorates an Essex Pub of the Year award that was presented by CAMRA back in 1992.

This building itself dates from the late 16th Century, and is thought to have originally been a farmhouse. At one time it was the home of the Haddock seafaring family, the most notable being Admiral Sir Richard Haddock.

Since then it has undergone many changes, the most notable back in 1855 when the entire back of the building was demolished to make way for the London to Southend railway. Further changes were made in 1937, when some Tudor beams were discovered, and again in 1944 when it was extended.

In the early 1850s, a club was formed here to help fisherman, living within one mile of the pub, who had fallen ill and were unable to work. Initially, the club was called the United Brethren, but soon afterwards it became known as the Billet Club.

Once every year, the members were treated to dinner and a social evening at the local rectory, and after the meal was completed, there would be dancing on the rectory lawn. The members were always well supplied with beer and it was not unusual for the fisherman to take the following week off work.

There has been much speculation about where this pub's name came from, and one school of thought connects the name with what was once a nearby beerhouse called the Billet. But the most likely explanation can be gained from the sign hanging outside; a billet is nothing more than a log of wood.

51 High Street, Leigh-on-Sea, SS9 2EP

Date visited

67

Rose & Crown, Writtle

Although built in the 16th century, not much of the original building now remains, except perhaps the cellars. The oldest parts still standing are at the back of the pub, whereas the front section was rebuilt in the early 1800s.

The earliest written documentation about the pub dates back to 1642, when it was named as the Rose and Crown in 'the towne of Writtle' and included in a legal deed by John Attwood of Grays Inn, on the occasion of his marriage to Elizabeth Young. This is the date painted on the front wall of the building.

In 1841, the alehouse was purchased by the Writtle Brewery Company and added to their estate of tied houses which by 1874 had expanded to 80 licensed premises. The landlord at the time, Samuel Lucking, was also a baker and there were ovens at the back of the premises for him to practice his other trade.

At one time, all staff who worked at the Writtle Brewery were entitled to drink as much beer as they wanted, a perk of the job that also applied to the deliverymen. It was fortunate for them that the dray horses knew their way back to the brewery, because it was not unknown for them to pull the cart all the way back from the last drop-off with the drayman blissfully sleeping in the back.

Sometime after 1902, George Rumsey took over as wheelwright and innkeeper, but within a year had to pass the business over to his son after his licence was taken away from him. This was because a customer, the worst for too much beer, had caused a disturbance outside that had attracted the attention of a local police officer. Unfortunately for the landlord there was a history of bad blood between him and this particular policeman, and seeing an opportunity to exact his revenge, the policeman took steps to have George's licence revoked.

The son, also named George, was to stay there for nearly fifty years, although he still found the time to go off and fight for his country in the First World War. He eventually retired in 1949.

At the start of his tenure, opening hours were not restricted and it was not unusual for George junior to be woken up, often before six in the morning, by the local blacksmith throwing stones at his bedroom window. He was wanting his pint before a days work sweating in the forge of his nearby smithy.

This pub stands next to a very pleasant village green, complete with mandatory duck pond, and in 1992 the owners at the time decided for no apparent reason that a change of name would be a good idea, and so re-branded the pub as The Inn on the Green.

Not surprisingly, this managed to upset many of the village residents who did not want this change to take place, but nevertheless the men-in-suits proceeded anyway. Not really the way for a pub to impress themselves on the local community and attract new customers. Fifteen years later things went full circle and the original name of the pub, the Rose and Crown, was reinstated. Although reverting to its original name, the now open-plan pub is very different from in the 1950s, when each of the three doors led to a separate room, and presumably a separate class of drinker.

57 The Green, Writtle, Chelmsford, CM1 3DT

Date visited

Swan, Little Totham

Dating from the 17th century, this former residential property eventually evolved into a beerhouse sometime during the 1800s.

The first recorded landlord was William Wager, who was listed as a poulterer and beer retailer, and lived there with his wife, Lydia and daughter Elizabeth. Elizabeth eventually married William Belcher, and by 1881 he had taken over as landlord from his then widowed mother-in-law.

During his time there, he sold one of his own concoctions that he called Gardener's Beer, although his customers probably had another name for it. One regular recalled it as the weakest drink he had ever tasted. It was, he said, nothing more than water drawn from the well in the garden, with some malt thrown in for flavour.

Mr Belcher seems to have got away with selling that, although he was not so fortunate with one of his sidelines as a coal-seller. He was called to appear before petty sessions in Little Totham accused of delivering his goods without a weighing machine.

About this time, the Court of the Lord of the Manor was regularly held at the Swan. The minutes from a sitting in 1909, record that four men each had to pay a sixpenny fine for defaulting on payments that were due to the lord for encroaching on his property.

The Swan remained as a beerhouse until as recently as the 1930s, when it first became fully licensed as a public house. At this time the licensing laws in this country were very strange, and included one rule that on Sundays, only customers who had travelled more than three miles to a pub were allowed to be served there. On that one day of the week, the men from Little Totham would leave for other nearby villages, only to pass on the way, residents of these same villages en-route to the Swan.

As recently as the mid 1990s, this pub was in serious danger of closing after its owners announced their intention to sell it for private housing. The local parish council then stepped in and made representations to the brewery to keep it as a local pub for the community. Eventually new people took over in June 1996, and since then the pub has never looked back. In 1999 they first gained an entry in the beer drinker's bible, the CAMRA good-beer guide.

The new management put their success down to the quality of their beer and the strong involvement they took with the local community. At the height of the French resistance to British beef, for example, they showed their support for local farmers by banning all French produce from the premises, even Beaujolais. They had a Bow Jollies festival instead.

In 2002, the supreme accolade came their way when they received an award from those same CAMRA people as the Great Britain National Pub of the Year. For some people this would have been a time for complacency, but that has never been on the agenda here and three years later they captured the same award again

School Road, Little Totham, CM9 8LB

Date visited

Griffin, Danbury

This building dates back to the 1500s, when it was a farmhouse called Peppers with 13 acres of land. It is first recorded as the Griffin in 1750, when at the time it belonged to Anthony Challis. In 1940 part of an earthenware mug or jug, dated from that period, was dug up in the garden, and clearly visible on this was his name, together with part of a drawing of an animal that may possibly have been a griffin.

The oak beams around the fireplace are old ships timbers, and the carved, 15th century woodwork is thought to have been taken from the church opposite after it was thrown out from there at the time of the reformation. There is a secret chamber over one of the bedrooms that can only be accessed through the chimney.

The Scottish novelist Sir Walter Scott, who wrote such classics as Ivanhoe and Rob Roy, is known to have frequently stayed here, and another famous visitor was the multi-talented artist, historian and novelist Joseph Strutt. In fact when Strutt died he left a novel unfinished, and as Scott's publishers thought it had some merit, they approached him and asked him to write the final two chapters. This he did although the book was not completed until six years after the death of Strutt.

Another celebrated guest was the charismatic, yet rather eccentric, Father Ignatius, who toured extensively preaching the benefit of monastic ways. He was described by Gladstone as one of the greatest orators of his day, and later became the self-appointed Abbot of Llanthony in Wales.

By 1801, when Joseph Myall owned the pub, its name had been slightly changed to the Griffin Head.

During an air raid in 1940, another discovery was found, concealed underneath the stairs by someone who was sheltering there. It was the fire-damaged will, dated 1789, of Thomas Bacon, who was described as a victualler and inn-holder of Danbury. In this he had left £10 to one son Abraham, £30 to his other son William, and the grand amount of £130 to his daughter, Mary. It's thought that this will was deliberately written to cause ill-feeling among his children, and it was probably one of them, or some other interested party, who had attempted to destroy it.

By the late 1800s, Danbury was becoming a tourist spot and the Griffin had not only stables for guest's horses, but also garaging facilities for the coming of the motor car. A sign in the window advertised the 'Cyclist Touring Club' which had been formed to promote bicycle-friendly establishments.

In 1914, Emil Rudin became the landlord and he remained there until 1947. At this time it was advertised as an important residential hotel with nine bedrooms, a lounge and a tearoom with fine views over the countryside. The views would have been quite spectacular as Danbury is one of the highest spots in Essex. It has been suggested that the Griffin is the highest pub in the whole of the county.

64 Main Road, Danbury, CM3 4DH

Date visited

Rose and Crown, Ashdon

One of the bars at the Rose and Crown, known as the Cromwell Room, is covered with elaborate wall paintings that were discovered when oak panelling was removed in the early 1900s. Legend has it that these were painted by Royalist monks from Bury, to help them while-away the days during their imprisonment here by Cromwellian forces. Their eventual fate is unknown, and it could be that their spirits still remain here because the building, and particularly this room, is reputed to be haunted.

On one wall is a large photo taken during World War Two of the landlord at the time and his wife, Mr and Mrs Moore. They are sharing a drink with an unnamed American airman who sadly was killed in action the very next day, when his plane was shot down over Germany. The futility of war.

Crown Hill, Ashdon CB10 2HB

Date visited

Axe and Compasses, Arkesden

The Axe and Compasses is an attractive, part-thatched, pub set in the unspoilt and picturesque village of Arkesden. The pub was originally built around 1650, although various additions have subsequently been made.

The weatherboarded section, which served as the stables until the 1920s, now houses the excellent restaurant, whilst on the other side of the main structure, the 'newer' nineteenth century extension acts as the public bar.

This is a fine example of how public bars used to be. And how they should be. There is a wooden floor with built-in wooden settles to sit on, and old barrels to use as tables. Probably nothing much has changed here over the last few decades, except perhaps some additions to the already numerous oddities and knick-knacks which adorn most of the walls. In fact the 1936, black and white, photo of an old car parked in front of the pub was most likely a photo of a brand new car when it was first hung on the wall.

Arkesden, Saffron Walden, CB11 4EX

Date visited

Five Bells, Colne Engaine

The Five Bells has a history going back to at least 1579, when Nicholas Buntyng was the innkeeper. A record of all the landlords since that date is now proudly displayed on one of the walls. The present building is thought to date from about 1760, and after being refaced in 1815, nothing much has changed externally since then.

On the 15th July 1840, an inquest was held here into the death of Henry Ringer, aged 16 years. It was decided that he had been 'killed by the boy Crick' but after further investigations it appears his death was not as murderous as first thought.

Apparently Ringer called out to James Crick and his friends that he would fight all four of them, one at a time. He started throwing skittle-pins at them, and this eventually led to fisticuffs between Crick and Ringer which left them both with severe injuries. At this stage, they both went home but by the next morning Ringer was dead and a few days later, James Crick pleaded guilty at Assizes to the charge of killing him.

However, the judge took a lenient view and said that because of the mitigating circumstances he was not disposed to deal severely with the prisoner. In fact he sentenced him to just one week's imprisonment.

Another inquest took place here in 1857, this time into the murder of local resident Isaac Butler. He died after being robbed of his money during a visit to Colchester. Whilst there, he had been seen taking a number of sovereigns from his pocket and this must have proved too tempting for his assailants. The verdict of the jury was 'wilful murder by persons or persons unknown'.

In the 1920s, Mr A Pitt was treasurer of The Five Bells Slate Club, a mutual benefit club formed to provide financial assistance to members in times of illness. At this time sick pay was not generally available. After any claims had been paid, the balance remaining would be shared out just before Christmas.

During the Second World War, a 'cigarette fund' was started by the landlord, Ben Goodwin and his wife Dolly. By the end of hostilities, over £230 had been raised for the benefit of around 40 customers serving in the armed forces.

At Christmas 1943, each recipient was sent a postal order, together with a photo of the interior of the taproom to remind them of home. One private, who was serving in the Middle East at the time, wrote back about the 'unspeakable joy' the gift had given to him.

The weather-boarded barn at the side of the pub, which is now the restaurant area, was once a butchers shop. Pigs were raised in the yard at the front, before its later conversion into the pub car park.

7 Mill Lane, Colne Engaine, CO6 2HY

| Date visited | |

Black Buoy, Wivenhoe

The original name for this pub was the Black Boy, which is a fairly common name for a pub, and is said to derive from the fact that King Charles II was so nicknamed on account of his black hair and swarthy appearance. Most pubs with this name date from the second half of the seventeenth century, and it's a reasonable to assume that the same applies here.

The first written record, however, was not until 1732, when the landlord was registered as John Hawes.

The spelling of the pub's name was changed in 1912, but not because of an early form of political correctness. The landlord at the time, Captain William Ennew, had recently retired from the Royal Navy and wanted something more nautical.

Another landlord with connections to the sea was Thomas Harvey who was landlord between 1832 and 1845. He was born in Wivenhoe in 1803 and after learning the carpentry trade as a teenager, combined the job of running the pub with that of being a boat builder.

He earned the reputation of being highly skilled in this trade and after leaving the pub, went on to build some fine yachts. The most famous of these was the 'Volante' which was one of the ships that took part in the Queen's Cup race around the Isle of Wight in 1851.

Queen Victoria herself was there to watch the yacht 'America' win the race and then presented a trophy to the winning team. They in turn announced that racing for the trophy would be an annual event and called it the Americas Cup, after the name of their victorious yacht. Over 150 years later, this is now the oldest trophy in the sporting world.

Thomas Harvey established a good family business in ship building, although his grandson resisted all efforts to join the business and instead chose a life on the stage. He was just as adept in this trade as his grandfather was in ship building, and in 1921 was knighted for his services to the acting profession.

As Sir John Martin-Harvey he was considered one of the last great romantic actors of the English theatre.

In the early years of the twentieth century one of the regulars here was the reverend Sinclair Carolin, a man with an opinion on everything, and full of righteousness and self-importance. In 1907, he officiated at the wedding of another former landlord's granddaughter, Bessie Goodwin, to Captain Caleb Fisher and afterwards gave them a present they surely treasured above all others, a signed photograph of himself.

Black Buoy Hill, Wivenhoe, CO7 9BS

Date visited

Bell, Castle Hedingham

This building dates from the latter half of the sixteenth century and was first mentioned by name as the Bell, in a map of 1592. There are many old beams hidden behind the plain, rendered façade, whilst the interior has been greatly changed and extended over the years.

There is a warren of separate rooms downstairs, with winding passages to link them together. The main bar is just a simple counter, and the beer is served by gravity dispense from the barrels standing on a shelf at the back.

Upstairs is the old assembly room that was used as a meeting place for local businessmen, as well as being the focal point for the social life of the district. During the 1700s, the Trustees of the Yeldham Grammar School would regularly meet at the Bell, and hop dealers would attend their annual hop-meeting here, followed by a dinner laid on by the landlord.

In addition to such meetings, the room was also used for musical evenings. One notice from 1794 advertised a concert of overtures,

80

concertos and songs starting at 7pm to be followed by a ball. Admission was five shillings, and those considering attending were also informed that 'the moon, being then at the full, would be favourable for those who come a distance'.

During this same period, theatrical companies would often visit and set up a stage in the yard at the back to perform their plays. An advertisement from 1777, promised a presentation on the next Saturday of a new comedy called 'The Maid of Oaks', followed two days later by an old classic, Romeo and Juliet.

The Bell later served as the meeting point for members of the local Hinckford Hundred Conservative Club, and such was the stature of this group, that proceedings of their meetings were often considered important enough to merit articles in The Times. They were regularly addressed by distinguished figures in their party, and no doubt it was well reported when Benjamin Disraeli, then joint-leader of the Tory opposition, addressed a rally here in 1849.

Until about this time, the Bell had been a stopping place for stagecoaches on the Bury to London route, a journey that could take up to twelve hours. But as with many other coaching inns, trade began to suffer as it fell victim to the advance of the railways.

Looking for alternative income, the landlord began to operate a post-chaise service to ferry passengers from remote outposts to and from the local train station. He also continued to act as an estate agent and property auctioneer, and presumably further supplemented his income when the pub was turned into a courthouse, every alternate Tuesday, for Petty Sessions to be held there.

10 St James Street, Castle Hedingham, CO9 2EJ

Date visited	

White Hart, Witham

The White Hart is an ancient coaching house, parts of which date back over 500 years. In Tudor times it housed the Trained Bands who were the fore-runners of the Home Guard. They were ever-ready to rush, at a moment's notice, to defend any part of the coast under attack. Inside one of the huge chimneys is a recess used in those days of old to dry the wood for making their bows and arrows.

Carved on one of the original oak beams is a rose inside a horseshoe, indicating that someone, perhaps a former landlord, took part in the spectacular Field of Cloth of Gold, in the year 1520. This was a meeting between Henry VIII and the King of France, and the extravaganza of feasts, balls, firework displays and other grandiose gestures eventually lasted three weeks. The effort to out-do each other eventually put a strain of the economies of both countries.

1n 1583, William Newman, who was described as a victualler and yeoman and had been a former parish constable, was hauled before the church court charged with adultery with his servant girl.

By 1654, Richard Swinburn was the innkeeper, and also postmaster, providing fresh horses for post boys who carried the mail in leather bags. He was involved in a dispute with the navy about a horse he had hired out to them.

In 1841, there was a long procession through the town to lay foundation stones for the new church. Afterwards, the 14 workmen involved were given dinner at the White Hart. There were also 200 buns distributed for the children.

Rebecca Cook, who was the landlady when this took place, liked to tell people that she was descended from Captain Cook, but there was in-fact no truth to this story.

The 'First Meeting of the Witham Labourers' was held here on 9th October 1845, and although meant to discuss serious matters, there were some light-hearted diversions. A competition, for example, to find the longest-serving domestic man to serve just one master or mistress.

An 1869 guide book mentioned the annual Witham Ball, held in January, which attracted distinguished gentlemen and their wives, from all over the country to the 'continued tradition of gentility'. For a while there was also a separate Tradesman's Ball.

At this time there was another pub, known as the White Hart Tap, at the back of this pub in Maldon Road. This was later known as the Half Moon, but seems to have disappeared by the turn of the 1900s. Perhaps it was replaced by a garage, because by 1902 petrol was sold on the premises. Clearly, the management here recognised the future importance of the motor car, and by 1908 members of the recently formed Royal Automobile Club were served 'by appointment'. There was also a billiards table for their further enjoyment.

Newland Street, Witham, CM8 2AF

Date visited

Kings Head, Pebmarsh

The central part of this building dates from around 1450, when the timbers used in its construction were taken from old sailing ships, some of which were said to date from the 12th century. The Kings Head was first officially licensed to sell beer under the General licensing Act of 1761.

Evidence of its use as an early hostelry have been found in the attic, where there were wooden cubicles to accommodate the passing drovers and waggoners. They would sleep on the floor unless prepared to pay a little more for the luxury of a hammock stretched between the beams.

Before the First World War there were lively scenes in the area around the Kings Head, usually culminating in an aftermath of bloody noses, when the Buggs family held their annual fair here. At the time there was a large stable block and brew house at the side of the pub although these have both since been demolished to make way for the car park.

The Street, Pebmarsh, Halstead, CO9 2NH

Date visited	

Rayleigh Arms (Riley's), Terling

Lord Rayleigh and his family lived in their Georgian country house, Terling Place, for many generations, and in 1825 his lordship, needing an overspill to accommodate guests, constructed this building to be used as an inn. It remained in the family until 1923 when it was sold to Ind Coope.

Although called the Rayleigh Arms, it is known locally as 'the Monkey' and is so called after one of the animals supporting the family coat of arms which has pride of place on the outside wall of the pub. This represents the Fitzgerald monkey, the first Lady Rayleigh being a member of that family. Legend has it that when their Irish castle caught fire in the 15th century, a pet monkey saved the infant heir by taking the child to the roof, and then bringing him down to safety.

In 1904, the regulars of this pub had good reason to celebrate when the third Lord Rayleigh, who had earlier in his career discovered the inert gas Argon, was awarded the Nobel Prize for physics.

1 Oak Hill, Terling, CM3 2PW

Date visited

The Peldon Rose, Peldon

April 22nd 1884, began as a pleasant, sunny day in the area around Peldon, a pretty village a few miles to the south of Colchester, but then, just after 9.00 in the morning everything suddenly changed. The area was struck by what is considered to be one of the most destructive earthquakes to ever hit Britain.

The epicentre for this quake was just in front of this fifteenth century pub, and not surprisingly it suffered much damage. Reports at the time stated that tiles were ripped from the roof, walls cracked and bulged and a large chimney stack broke through the centre of the roof, crashed through the floors and smashed into the cellar.

By the time that this had been repaired, and some sense of normality returned to the village, the pub was once again under threat. This time by the German zeppelins that were attacking England during World War One.

On one particular night in 1916, one of the raiders started losing gas, and fearing that his crew would be lost at sea if attempting to return home, the captain decided to land. It was in the Peldon area that his men put their feet back on terra firma, and after setting fire to their airship they set off for Colchester to surrender at the military garrison.

However, on their way they met an off-duty police sergeant who happened to be in the area and he took them into custody.

The main body of the airship contained about two million cubic feet of hydrogen, and so the fire turned into quite an explosion. Fragments were blown in all directions and some which landed in the vicinity of the Rose were until a few  years ago wall-mounted in the bar. The picture above was taken at the time, and the immense size of the craft can be judged by comparing it to the house on the left of the picture.

In the period after the end of this war and before the start of the next one, the landlady, Mrs Pullen, claimed that the pub was haunted. She said that the ghost of a Roman centurion had appeared before her, presumably in his battledress.

Like many waterside pubs, the Rose had close links with smuggling, or the free-trade as some preferred to call it, and took advantage of a very unique place to hide contraband from the inquisitive eyes of the customs officials. This was a large well, hidden in the middle of the pond beside the pub. Weighted barrels of spirits were rowed out on a boat and lowered down on ropes, until the revenue men had completed their searches and the coast was clear.

Today things are much more peaceful in the area, and hopefully visitors now can relax in one of the most comfortable pubs in the area, fairly safe from the risk of Zeppelin attacks or the threat of another earthquake.

Colchester Road, Peldon, CO5 7QJ

Date visited

Woolpack, Coggeshall

The Woolpack dates from the 15th century and started life as a home for one of the prosperous wool merchants who lived in the town. By the 16th century, it had became a hostelry for those in the same business, but when the wool trade started to decline, it reverted back to a private house

In 1665, it was purchased by Thomas Lowrey who had previously been the vicar of the local church. He had been expelled a few years earlier, because of disagreements over his puritanical views, and thereafter he used the premises to preach to independent congregations. A blue plaque on the wall commemorates this.

Things usually go in cycles and by 1708 it had once again become an inn, although for a short time it was known as the Woolpack and Punchbowl.

Over its lifetime the outside of this pub has also undergone many changes, and by the early part of the last century much of the 'old fashioned' stud work had been covered by plaster. However, by the 1930s fashion had gone full circle and as part of a major refurbishment this plaster was removed, thus returning the exterior to its original state.

Whilst carrying out this work, some hammering on an internal wall revealed it to be hollow in places, and so a decision was made to remove it. Behind this boarding, blame for which can be laid at a previous owner, a magnificent brick fireplace was discovered.

By this time, the floor of the main dining area sloped by as much as eight inches from its centre to its side walls, which must have made the pleasure of eating there a precarious occupation. During the 1950s, when the novelty value had worn off, the present false, floor was laid.

Along the wall in the back bar there are a dozen or more paintings and drawings of this pub, all from different stages of its evolution. Some show the row of cottages that were subsequently knocked down to facilitate the car-park. There's also a 1955 photograph from the renowned Francis Frith collection, and after taking this the photographer probably popped inside for a well-deserved glass of refreshment. That would explain the snap he also took of the interior which now hangs, slightly surreally, in the same spot where he stood to take it fifty years earlier.

During the 1960s, there was a separate restaurant upstairs in what is known as the King Post room. In here a large, ornately carved wooden post dominates the room.

Woolpack, 61 Church Street, Coggeshall, CO6 1UB

Date visited

Paul Pry, Rayleigh

Originally erected as a private house, the oldest part of this building dates back to around 1550. Various additions were then made before it first opened as an inn, name unknown, about 100 years later.

The name Paul Pry originates from a comedy by John Poole, which was first performed in 1825 at the Haymarket theatre, London. The title role was that of an amiable busybody unable to mind his own business. His favourite phrase was "I hope I don't intrude", but actually he spent his whole life interfering with the affairs of other people.

The name stuck and has applied to busybodies and eavesdroppers ever since. In Victorian times, there was even a scandal-mongering news sheet published under the same name.

Many old pubs are reputed to have a secret tunnel somewhere on the premises, and the Paul Pry is no exception. Supposedly it ran underneath the road, from the pub to the police station opposite, and condemned prisoners were moved along this route on their way to the nearby gallows. This site is now occupied by another pub, the Travellers Joy.

The census of 1851 lists Thomas Livermore as the landlord. He lived there with his wife and six children, and also on the premises were no less than eighteen lodgers. Their various occupations included sailor, agricultural labourer, hatter, tin-man and watchmaker. Facilities were also made available, at no charge, for assorted vagrants and tramps to sleep in a barn which ran alongside the inn. They had the pleasure of wooden benches, with straw for bedding, and a connecting hatch enabled them to purchase beer for 1 penny a pint or 'drips' for half the price.

Another previous landlord was Albert French, a retired policeman who had previously pounded the beat, not far away in Hadleigh. When he took over in 1906, he not surprisingly maintained strict discipline and discouraged foul language by his customers. At this time there were three staircases in the building. One was used by the better-off visitors for access to their well-appointed rooms, and the second was for staff and family. Mr

French did not allow his children to use the third staircase as he said it was for tallymen and they brought bugs and fleas with them.

During the First World War, a company of pioneers were billeted in a nearby shed, and as they were restricted from purchasing alcohol, they sought the help of one of the local lads to buy some for them. The boy lied to this same landlord that he was collecting the ale for his father, but after a while the ex-policeman thought the amounts ordered were suspicious and so cut off their supply.

In 1935, the Paul Pry ran a competition for green-fingered people in the area, who grew their own produce. Among the prizes awarded was one to the grower of the longest runner bean. When one competitor held up his entry there was no doubting that it had won by several inches at least, but after he had left with his winnings in his pocket, it was discovered that he had secured first prize by craftily grafting two beans together.

14 High Road, Rayleigh, SS6 7AA

Date visited	

The Marquis, Colchester

The Marquis is renowned for the exceptional examples of 16th century carvings that can be found in various parts of the building. One giant beam displays various animals and birds, together with some fiery dragons, and rests on posts of giant carved figures dressed in 16th century costume.

Unfortunately, this is in what is now the public bar, complete with pool table, although in more genteel times it used to be the billiards room.

Another interesting feature, which can be found over the fireplace in the same room, is a colourful bas-relief that was adapted from a design by a former mayor of the town, Sir W Gurney Benham. It portrays twenty or so notable people connected with the history of the town, all sitting down to the famous Colchester Oyster Feast.

Built around 1520 as a private house, it is not known exactly when these premises first became an inn. Certainly it was described as an alehouse in 1753, although it was then known as The Crown.

In 1770, the name was changed to the Marquis of Granby, to commemorate the death that year of General John Manners, who held that title, and was commander-in-chief of the British troops during the seven year war against France which started in 1756.

The Marquis took an unusual concern for the welfare of the troops who served under him, and after the war he provided funds for many of the disabled officers to buy pubs. Out of respect they named their pubs after him, thus making this a very popular name for such establishments throughout the country.

He also gave rise to what is still today a well known saying. In his day it was usual for men to wear wigs, even in battle, but this found no favour with him. Thus the phrase was coined 'to go into something bald-headed'.

This pub underwent a major refurbishment in 1914 when a more recent brickwork front was removed, and the original oak framing exposed and renovated. At the same time, the inside of the building was also, where possible, restored to its original condition.

They say that history repeats itself and in 1997 it was refurbished once again. This time, however, it was decided to alter the name to just the Marquis, and any reference to the old chap was removed.

However, he's had the last laugh on them because his picture, bald head and all, still adorns the pub sign that hangs outside the building. He probably knows that when its next refurbishment falls due, the name of the pub is likely to be changed again, and at that time his full title will probably be restored.

24-25 North Hill, Colchester, CO1 1EG

Date visited

Bell, Tolleshunt Major

The Bell was built around 1540, and may have been put up by Stephen de Beckingham to serve as an alehouse and hostel for his newly acquired estate. His family were large landowners, and to reflect their status in the community, the pub also became known as the Beckingham Bell.

Fred Offord and his wife, Bessie, took over the tenancy in the mid 1920s and remained here for over thirty years. Bessie played the organ at the local church every Sunday, and as she couldn't be in two places at one time, opening of the pub was delayed until about 12:15pm to allow her time to cycle back from this other job. She enjoyed a game of dominoes and would play every night, when not knitting socks for her customers at a charge of one shilling a pair.

Beckingham Street, Tolleshunt Major, CM9 8LL

Date visited	

Thatchers, Hatfield Heath

Standing inside this fine pub it's hard to visualise the building back around 1580, when it was first constructed as nothing more than a barn. It then became a smithy before being converted into four cottages. During the 1800s, it became a beerhouse called the Waggon and Horses, and in 1869, when the sale of alcohol was brought under stricter control, it converted into a recognised inn.

On Boxing Day 1946, some of the regulars would have joined the large crowd at the nearby football ground to watch the local team take on a Prisoner of War XI. They expected to see an easy victory for the home side but the German team contained several international players in their ranks, and eventually won by a resounding 11-0.

Sometime around 1985 the pub's name was changed to Thatchers.

Stortford Road, Hatfield Heath, CM22 7DU

Date visited

The George, Shalford

The building now known as the George dates back to the 15th century. It is heavily timbered inside with many low beams, and has a large inglenook fireplace that had been covered up and completely forgotten until it was re-discovered in 1969. This was while some renovation work was being carried out. Strangely, another fireplace, sharing the same chimney, was later found during the 1980s.

The George is the sole survivor in the village where there was, one hundred years ago, no less than five public houses. This however, was the only one with the status of being called an inn, and this meant that any traveller could demand a bed for the night, and breakfast the next morning, providing, of course, that he could afford the going rate. As an inn it also meant that dead bodies could be taken inside the premises.

The earliest recorded licensee is George Sharpington, who ran the pub in 1724 and paid an annual rent for the premises of £7. By 1790, when Ruth Abel was in charge, the rent had increased to £10 a year.

When Thomas Bearman took over in 1866, the lease was for the pub together with 'the piggeries belonging to the establishment'.

An unusual use was found for the snug bar during the 1970s, when for a while it also served as a doctor's waiting room. This was at the time when Dr Goudry solved the problem of his Shalford patients being cut off from their GP, by operating a mobile surgery from his motorised caravan. He also used this to dispense any medicines that he prescribed.

Whilst the patients were waiting for their turn to be seen, the landlord's wife was happy to make coffee for them. However, it's said that some of them had other ideas about their choice of refreshment.

Later, when Les and Joan Burton were running the pub, the Ancient Order of Bowler Hatters was formed. This started because one of their customers used to visit the pub every Sunday lunchtime, resplendent in his best suit, and politely raise his hat to any ladies he met there. Gradually other regulars joined in this ritual of gentlemanly conduct until the club had up to 15 members.

Subsequently, any member not raising his hat whenever a lady entered or left the pub was levied with a fine to pay. The money collected throughout the year was added to by raffles, dart matches and other fund-raising activities and used at the end of the year to buy Christmas hampers for the old folk in the village.

After the club had been running for just one year, no less than 34 such hampers were distributed, and Anglia Television sent a film crew along to broadcast the event. Later on fame for this club spread much further a field and in 1972, the recently-crowned Miss World, Australian Belinda Green, visited the pub to meet with the members and have her photograph taken alongside them.

The Street, Shalford, Braintree, CM7 5HH

Date visited

Star, Ingatestone

The Star dates from around 1480, and was originally built as a private house named Bramwood. By 1560, the property was leased to Thomas Sturgeon who paid rent to the owner of one shilling per annum.

The first official records of the building begin in the reign of Charles I, when it was conveyed to Jane Aylett in a deed dated February 20th 1631. It was at this time that it became a pub called the White Horse. It was extensively modernised in the early 1640s, perhaps 1641 to be exact, for that is the year, together with the initials G E M, carved into the rough beam over the fireplace.

Over the next couple of centuries the building was used for a number of different trades. In 1749 it was leased to Edward White, the local butcher, and he set up his slaughterhouse at the back. One hundred years later it was a bakery. The original old oven has now been rediscovered and restored.

Eventually it joined the estate of pubs owned by local brewer Walter Gray, when he purchased it in 1883 for a price of £530.

In the early 20th century, horse fairs were held at the end of the lane that runs beside this pub. Unfortunately, along with the dealers and drovers who came from all over England and Wales, it also attracted the sort of roughs who would fight like dogs, and steal anything they could get their hands on. The landlord at the time didn't want them inside his pub, but was nevertheless quite happy to take their money. To do this he opened the small window at the side and passed the beer out to them. For obvious reasons the pub acquired the nickname of The Hole in the Wall.

In more recent times there have been some strange happenings at the Star. In 1956, two sisters, who had paid to spend the night there, reportedly left in a hurry after the lights in their room turned themselves on and off, and their door repeatedly opened and closed.

Another tale concerns that of the ghost of a dog that was said to haunt the premises in the early 1960s. Apparently, the bristles of any dog that was led there would immediately go up, and he would growl or shrink back. The landlord at the time knew instinctively when he first set foot there that it was not the spirit of a man, because he said, he could sense and almost see a black dog, teeth bared and blazing with hatred.

This description exactly matches that of a dog that lived on the premises from 1900 until 1914 or so. He fought every dog for miles around and was never beaten. He was also thought responsible for killing half the cats in the village.

The story goes that after he died the stuffed head of this beast was hung from one of the beams in the corner, and it was only after it was removed from the premises that the trouble began. However, when the ghastly object was located, and restored to its original spot, canine harmony was immediately restored.

45 High Street, Ingatestone, CM4 9ED

Date visited

Chequers, Roxwell

Originally built in the 17th century, the Chequers has since that time been considerably altered and added to. It was first mentioned by name in 1715, when it formed part of the estate of Francis Perry and bequeathed to his wife Margaret for the term of her life. Thereafter it was to go to his grandson, William Nash.

It was first registered as an alehouse in 1770, when the licensee was Thomas Milbank. By the time that the next register was published, in 1824, Thomas Gower was in charge.

Henry Earnshaw became landlord in 1896, and moved in with his wife and four children. In addition to work duties he also found time to act as clerk to the parish council, and was also a stone-walling opening bat for the local cricket team. At one time he was joined in the team by the local vicar who was, by all accounts, a batsman of near-county standard.

In 1906, an inquest was held at the Chequers into the sad death of a young boy, not even nine years old, named Charlie Bert Brown. He had worked for the local farmer, and one day just fell asleep whilst leading a horse and wagon, and was run over and killed by it.

Even at this tender age he had been doing this job for two years, both in the morning and after school in the evening. A verdict of accidental death was recorded, and the foreman added a rider that children of that age should not be employed in work of that description. Another member of the jury asked "Do you think, Mr Coroner, if there is any possibility of there ever being a law to make this sort of thing illegal?"

Following the death of Henry Earnshaw in 1929, his son Frederick, who had been just one year old when he originally moved there with his family, took over as landlord. He, in turn, stayed until 1958 thus completing over sixty years service by the same family.

Just as his father had run the business during the First World War, so did Frederick run it throughout the Second. During this conflict the village blacksmith acted as Air-Raid Warden and was based here because there was a telephone on site.

Later in the war, the Home Guard were stationed at the Chequers, and every night four men reported there for duty. Armed and in uniform they stood ready to repel any German invasion.

Following Frederick's death in 1958, his widow stayed for a further five years until 1963, when the aptly named Thomas Brewer became the next landlord. By this time ownership of the pub had been sold by Russell's Brewery and it had become part of the Truman's estate.

The Street, Roxwell, Chelmsford, CM1 4PD

Date visited	

George and Dragon, Epping

This old coaching inn was first licensed in the 17th century, when it was just known as the George. Appropriately, the first recorded landlord was named George Dey, and he was subsequently succeeded by his son, also called George, in 1668.

By 1795, William Ingram, a brandy merchant, owned the building, and at some time during that year he paid a local tradesman the sum of eight shillings to have the advertising signboard outside painted and gilded.

In 1830, whilst Mary Thurgood was the landlady, an amusing event happened here which was eventually reported in some of the London newspapers. This involved Thomas Godfrey, the master of the local workhouse, who was seen leaving the inn accompanied by a woman with a lead tied around her neck. It was his intention to sell her by auction and in fact he received a bid of 2/6d. However, before he the transaction could be completed, a police constable arrived on the scene and charged him with selling goods and chattels without a licence. Eventually Godfrey was hauled before the justices but the case was then thrown out of court because, they decreed, a wife could not be considered the goods or chattels of a husband.

Throughout all of this no one seemed to give any regard to the feelings of the unfortunate woman, although there was some suspicion at the time that the whole event had been deliberately staged.

A few years after this occurred, the inn was purchased by Edward Ind, who then changed its name to the George and Dragon. Subsequently, Mr Ind went into partnership with George Coope and together they formed the brewing giant Ind, Coope & Co.

In 1898, whilst Robert Lee was the landlord, a burning log fell from the grate and the resulting fire completely gutted one of the upstairs bedrooms. Fortunately, the newly-equipped local fire brigade brought it rapidly under control and averted what could have been a potential disaster.

Five years later and the delightfully-named Gaius Stubbings had taken over as landlord. He already knew the place well, because as a young lad he had helped with the bottling of lemonade and ginger beer in the mineral water works situated at the back of the pub. It was during his tenure that the owners decided, in 1905, to plaster over the Georgian brick frontage

During a refurbishment in 1981, an old chimney breast that had previously been bricked-up was reopened. Inside was a hand-written note dated 1904, together with a photograph of the afore-mentioned Gaius Stubbings.

In 1996, a storm broke out when new owners announced their intention of changing the name of the pub to the Forest & Firkin. Many local people did not want this to happen, but the change went ahead anyway. However, this was only a temporary setback for the pub and during the year 2000 it reverted back to its correct name.

208 High Street, Epping, CM16 4AQ

Date visited

Kings Head, Rochford

Legend has it that sometime around the year 1620, the Lord of the Manor returned home unexpectedly from fighting battles overseas and heard the sound of men whispering outside his house. On listening closer he realised that it was his tenants talking, and furthermore that they were plotting to kill him. At the time he pretended not to hear, but later, just to cause them inconvenience, he ordered that they must meet every year, at midnight on the first Wednesday after Michaelmas, and answer their names to a roll call. He decreed that anyone not attending would be heavily fined.

This started the tradition of the Whispering Court that lasted for over two hundred and fifty years, although it eventually changed into just a social occasion. In these later days the participants, before walking to the appointed spot, would enjoy a grand dinner at the Kings Head, washed down with a large bowl of punch. However, by about 1897, this age old custom died out, due to the disturbance that the drunken revellers caused in the town.

11 West Street, Rochford, SS4 1BE

Date visited	

The Mitre, Wickham Bishops

The name of this pub was changed from the Carpenters Arms to this more ecclesiastical title in the mid 1890s, possibly to acknowledge that the village was once owned by the Bishops of London.

Constructed in the early 1600s as a row of cottages, it seems that at some later stage just two of them were converted into the pub. There was a public bar and saloon bar together with a 'jug and bottle' in the middle for off-sales. It was much later that the pub encroached into the third, left-hand cottage.

Carved across one of the old beams in the public bar is the cryptic inscription: 'Tho hearts of oak be so stout, keep me dry I will last him out'. Alongside this is written the date of 1771.

During some rebuilding in 1975, an old fireplace was uncovered, with some old newspaper cuttings inside it, along with a few clay pipes. These are now displayed in a glass frame on the wall. Also found was part of an envelope, which according to the postmark on the penny red had been posted from Stevenage on 12 October 1868.

2 The Street, Wickham Bishops, Witham, CM8 3NN

Date visited

Britannia, Barking

The Britannia is thought to have been built as a beerhouse around the year 1848. The name of the first landlord is unknown, although by the time of the census three years later, John Stubbings was listed as a beer retailer and widower. He was living there with his two young daughters, Mary and Caroline.

The building has since been altered several times. The first occasion was sometime after 1874, when during the tenancy of Alexandre MacAlister it was extensively rebuilt.

After being purchased by Walter Kitson in 1887, the Britannia was effectively redesigned yet again ten years later, this time by the Victorian architect Frederick W. Ashton. In keeping with the trademark that he used on many other of his creations, the busty caryatids reminiscent of a ship's prow were added to the outside walls.

These act as a reminder of Barking's seafaring days, although no reminder or explanation is required as to why the pub has since then always been known locally as 'The Tits'.

Singer and superstar Billy Bragg was born in Barking, and once wrote that he considered this pub to be his local. He said he could remember once, when the pub was undergoing redecoration, that someone decided to paint the nipples of the gable girls an enticing shade of rouge. Although as schoolchildren they could appreciate the artistic merit on display, he didn't think this was an opinion shared by the members of the Tanner Street Tabernacle across the road.

"The church" he said "has now gone but the bare breasts of the Britannia remain, covered in nothing more than several coats of Dulux All-Weather Off-White paint". He always did have such a way with words!

Following Walter Kitson's death in 1906, the pub was run by his widow Jane, and then by George who was one of their seven children. The family retained an interest in the pub for nearly 80 years and George was still there when it was altered again during the 1930s.

In 1955, the family finally got round to repairing damage caused during World War Two.

As recently as 1965 it was sold to the south-London based Youngs brewery. At this time it became their only tied pub in Essex, although a few more have subsequently been added.

Although situated in Essex, the Britannia is a typical east London boozer, with a large lounge and separate, more basic, public bar. It regularly wins awards from CAMRA for the quality of its beer.

1 Church Road, Barking IG11 8PR

Date visited	

Red Lion, Billericay

The Red Lion is one of the oldest buildings in Billericay, originally being part of a 15th century private house called Merchants. By 1593 it was known as the Lion when the Elizabethan mapmaker, Ralph Aggar, included it on a map of the area. At the time, Jacob Warne was the tenant.

By 1769, Abraham Thresher was the landlord and was advertising in the local paper that he had 'lately set up a very neat and genteel post-chariot, and humbly hoped the ladies and gentlemen in the neighbourhood would favour him with their commands'.

The annual meeting of the Court Leet and Baron were held here, presided over by the lords of the manor, the Petre family. At these meetings, which took place at the start of Whitsun week, the affairs of Billericay were settled for the following year. Decisions made included the appointment of the Constable and other officials, including an ale-tester.

This throwback to feudal times continued to be held until the 1920s, probably because, their tasks completed, everyone spent the rest of the week celebrating in the time-honoured fashion.

In 1804, the inn was acquired by a firm of brewers, who owned it for about ten years before dividing the building into two separate parts. One part was retained as the pub and the other was sold off as a private house. It is now a shop.

During celebrations for Queen Victoria's Diamond Jubilee in 1897, tables were set out in the street outside the Red Lion. A whole ox was roasted nearby, and the meat was available to all comers free of charge.

A few years later in 1904, when a general meeting of the Billericay Sparrow and Rat Club was held here, it was announced that 'during the season' the members had destroyed 3,024 sparrows' eggs.

The Red Lion was used as Police Headquarters during investigations into the 1927 murder of P.C. Gutteridge. His body had been found at the side of the road with his helmet and notebook beside him and his pencil still in his hand. Eventually, those responsible were captured and executed, and afterwards one Sunday paper carried the headline 'Hanged by a microscope' to reflect the fact that microscopic examination of the cartridge cases had provided the crucial evidence.

This was one of the earliest cases solved by what we now call ballistics.

In it's time, activities carried on at this inn include being an agent for an assurance company, running a Post and Excise Office and in 1874 it was an Inland Revenue office. Now it is just a very good pub.

113 High Street, Billericay, CM12 9AJ

Date visited

Kings Head, North Weald

The Kings Head has served as the village alehouse for the good people of North Weald since at least 1592. A licence that was granted to the property in that year still survives.

The building was probably erected about 50 years before this, and it's reputed that ships timbers from the navy of Henry VIII were used in its construction. This became common practice when the fleet fell into decline and builders near naval dockyards found that salvaging these old timbers was a cheaper option than purchasing new ones. Some of the beams bear prefabrication marks that could have been made by old shipwrights.

Some of the doors in this pub are no more than five feet high, and this only partly reflects the fact that people were a lot shorter in earlier times. Another reason they seem so low is because the pub has sunk over the years. It is also very crooked, with beams leaning and sagging in all directions, possibly because the foundations have been weakened by a stream that runs nearby. Surveys also show that the crookedness is getting worse, although there is no imminent danger of collapse.

One of the rooms, known as the Squire's Room, does though have a high ceiling and is reminiscent of a small, mediaeval banqueting hall. However on closer inspection it can be seen that the original ceiling has been the removed and the room is now really two storeys high. The doors halfway up the walls give this secret away.

This pub stands on the old London to Colchester road, and as an indication of how fashions change, even in pubs, the entire front was plastered over during the 18th century. This was to create a more modern image to passing travellers.

This false facade remained until 1927, when it was removed and the original frontage saw daylight once again. At the same time, the north-easterly, left-hand side of the pub was added. This extension blends in perfectly with the rest of the building and is hardly discernable apart from the fact that it is much straighter.

During the last war this pub was very popular with the airmen based at the nearby airfield, and after it suffered some serious bomb damage it was suspected that the Luftwaffe was targeting it for special treatment.

One bomb fell so close that it blew out much of the wattle and daub in-filling, but the massive timbers themselves never budged. Proof not only of their strength, but also of the carpentry skills of the men who worked on them back in those Tudor times. Because of labour and material shortages, the pub remained in that skeleton state for some time and local wags, who thought it reminiscent of an animal carcass, renamed it the Filleted Inn.

8 High Road, North Weald Bassett, CM16 6BU

| Date visited | |

Sun, Dedham

Built in the early part of the 16th century, the Sun was originally a private house set in a street lined with the residences of prosperous clothiers. According to one set of deeds, it was at one time called Bards although this may be a 17th century spelling mistake of an earlier name of Wards.

During its heyday in coaching times, the Sun stood on the main highway for passengers travelling from Ipswich and East Anglia to Maldon, Colchester and Harwich, and took full advantage of this location to attract their business. An advertisement in The Ipswich Journal of 1766 described the accommodation as 'good bed chambers, with a good kitchen, bar and proper conveniences'. It also promised 'a brew-office with good cellars and wine vaults.'

One unusual feature is the exceptionally tall coach-arch. It's possible that at some stage the inn took over the neighbouring cottage, and then roofed over the lane between to give the impression of just one building. This porch-way was high enough not to cause any problems for coachmen when driving through in their coaches and wagons piled high with baggage.

There is a small shop in the 'second' building that has, over the centuries, been used for a variety of purposes. During those coaching days it was a barbers and also a place where gentlemen could have any necessary repairs or maintenance carried out to their wigs. Subsequently it became a curio and antique shop, then a butchers, until by 2007 it was selling locally-grown fruit and vegetables.

Before the local assembly rooms were built, the Sun was a focal point for a variety of social events and meetings. This included being the before-and-after venue for bowls teams, whose matches took place in the collage grounds across the road.

In 1824, the Society for the Protection of Property against Arson and Robbery was formed and their meetings were held here or just down the road at the Marlborough Head.

There are a number of letting rooms here, one of which is called the Elsa room, but anyone planning to stay should first be aware that this was not a name picked at random. Legend has it that a serving wench of that name was employed here, until being branded a witch during the period when Matthew Hopkins was making a fortune in that line of work. Subsequently she was burned at the stake in the courtyard at the rear, the last person in the county, it's said, to meet with such a fate.

Her ghost now haunts the premises, and has been seen at various times ever since in the bedrooms and on the staircase. It's usually during busy lunchtimes when she is spotted, often wearing different clothes, but always with her hands held to her face, weeping.

High Street, Dedham, CO7 6DF

Date visited

Lamarsh Lion, Lamarsh

Originally a private lodge called Brownings, and used as a base for hunting wild boar, there has been an inn on this site since as far back as 1305.

There is a joke around here that anyone who visits this pub on a Sunday fulfils their Christian duty for the week. This is because the bar counter has been fashioned from what was once a church pulpit. It is carved with the inscription 'To the Greater Glory of God and in loving memory of Alfred Bradley Yorke, for many years a treasurer of this church, entered into rest 19th May 1907'.

Nothing more is known about the Mr Yorke, because it was not actually in Lamarsh that he carried out his good work. In fact the pulpit, together with some well-worn pews, was obtained from a church in Worcestershire, and installed here by the landlord of the day during the 1960s.

Bures Road, Lamarsh, CO8 5EP

Date visited

Ferry Boat Inn, North Fambridge

If you are in the area around North Fambridge and hear talk about the FBI, do not look around for American spies in raincoats and dark glasses. This is just the name given by the locals to their village pub, the Ferry Boat Inn.

The pub is believed to date from the late 15th or early 16th century, and was originally built as two or possibly three cottages. The exact date it became an inn is unclear, although records indicate that it was certainly called this name by the year 1659.

The ferry referred to in the name formed part of the general business of the pub, and carried passengers between here and South Fambridge on the opposite bank of the River Crouch. The licensee often acted as both innkeeper and ferryman, and although this service has now closed, the ghost of one former operator still remains on the premises and reputedly haunts the inn.

Ferry Road, North Fambridge, CM3 6LR

Date visited

Red Lion, Kirby-le-Soken

The main chimney stack of the Red Lion has been dated back to the early 1500s, and this would suggest that the building was constructed sometime during the reign of Henry VIII.

The pub is reputedly haunted by the ghost of a former servant who used to reside on the 2nd floor. This area is now just used as attics, but the sound of his heavy footsteps have been heard in the past, walking across the ceiling below. To keep him company, the ghosts of two small children have occasionally been seen, and more often just heard, playing in one of the upstairs front rooms.

The various creeks and islands in the stretch of water on which this village was originally founded were an ideal spot for smugglers to operate. Men from this pub were certainly implicated, and it was always rumoured that a tunnel existed from here down to the water's edge. Evidence of this was supposedly found as recently as 1999 whilst work was being carried out to extend the kitchens.

The village of Kirby is notorious for the riots of 1830, when farm workers, angered by the loss of jobs and reduced wages caused by the introduction of threshing machines, took matters in their own hands and set off to destroy the offending equipment. Eventually the crowd, which numbered two to three hundred, marched to the Red Lion where they faced the farmers and landowners who had gathered there to meet with them.

The farmers were handed a list of demands which they appeared to agree to, and the seemingly triumphant mob could do little more than disperse and go home. However, a couple of days later the ringleaders were rounded up and taken in chains to Chelmsford jail, where after a short trial, they were found guilty and sentenced to up to 14 years transportation to the other side of the world. At the time, no thought was given to the wives and children that these previously law-abiding men were forced to leave behind.

Whilst some major work was being carried out after the end of World War Two, an ancient cannonball was found in the foundations. At the same time, a couple of storeys higher up, a priest hole was discovered behind a fireplace in the private living quarters.

Before this refurbishment, there was a tap-room where the beer served to customers was poured straight from casks standing on tables behind the bar. However, this was jettisoned to make way for the restaurant.

In one bar there is a corner unit housing an excellent collection of old lead soldiers. Some of these are wearing uniforms that were probably in fashion when the corner unit was constructed, during the 1700s. For over 200 years since then it's been used as a showcase for successive landlord's favourite collections.

32 The Street, Kirby-le-Soken, CO13 0EF

Date visited

Castle, Hadleigh

During the mid 1600s, the land on which this inn now stands was sold by a farmer from Leigh to Helen Taylo, a widow who lived in Smithfield. For this she paid the sum of fifty shillings, which is less than the cost now of a pint of beer.

There had previously been cottages on the site, but she had a new building constructed and by 1664 this was to become the Boar's Head Inn. This name was often used to represent hospitality from the custom of serving a boar's head in feasts.

Sam King was landlord at the time but he fell foul of the law and was prosecuted for 'profaning the Lord's day by drawing beer in time of divine service'. Considering the inn was almost opposite the church it was surprising that he thought he could get away with it.

By 1775, the inn's name had changed to the Blue Boar, perhaps a reference to a type of local boar. This change took place whilst Richard and Sally Mitchell were the licensees. It was not until 1823, when John and Sally Warne had taken over, that it was given its present title of the Castle.

By this time, the surrounding area had become quite notorious as a haunt for local smugglers. Also many ex-soldiers, demobilised following the end of the Napoleonic war, moved here with their families and then turned to crime when no other means of income was available.

Legend has it that a tunnel or secret passage runs from this pub to Hadleigh castle, nearly one mile away. It was said that contraband goods came into the village via that underground route. However, no evidence has been found to support this, and considering it would have been a major engineering feat to construct such a tunnel, it's probably safe to let this remain as just a legend.

At the rear of the pub there was a well, which was in daily use until the early 1900s, when running water was first introduced into the area. There were also stables for the horses.

During the First World War, another type of four-legged guest was housed here when some army officers, billeted nearby, used the stables to house their regimental mascot, a white goat. This was to the great delight of local schoolchildren.

In 1924, whilst William Sheavill was landlord, the premises were considerably extended with the addition of the fourth gable, and five years later the Castle was purchased by the London brewers, Charringtons.

With the passing of the age of horse transport, the stables became obsolete and by 1940 they were replaced with garages. These in turn were pulled down twenty years later to enlarge the car park. In 1991 the pub was again further extended with the construction of a larger conservatory at the rear of the building.

High Street, Hadleigh, SS7 2PB

Date visited

Ye Olde Kings Head, Chigwell

The Kings Head was originally built during the reign of Henry VIII as an administrative centre for Epping Forest. It also served as a guest house for any government officials who were visiting the area.

Queen Elizabeth I slept here whilst on a hunting expedition to the forest, and it's said that she woke the next morning in a foul temper, and boxed the ears of a groom who had been clumsy while assisting her to mount her horse. The mounting block she stood on remains, even now, as one of a pair outside the door.

It then became home for the Court of Attachment, and anyone convicted here of poaching would expect to be severely dealt with. This was also known as the 'Forty-Days' Court because of the intervals in which it sat. Later, Verderers Courts, which dealt with lesser offences committed within the forest land, were held here until 1855. This court originally sat in Chelmsford but was moved here because it was said to be a more central position, although the fact that the verderers kept their wine cellar here may have been the real reason.

After that it seems to have served as the village school for a while, before becoming an important coaching house on the London to Norwich road.

One customer here was the notorious highwayman Dick Turpin, who it's said, began his criminal career in the area poaching deer from nearby Epping Forest. He would often pop in for a pot of ale, and take the opportunity to glean information about any wealthy travellers who he could later relieve of their valuables.

In later times, Charles Dickens was a regular guest. He often stayed here during the 1840s, and it's generally recognised that it was on this pub that he based his description of the Maypole in his novel Barnaby Rudge. He described it vividly, if a little inaccurately, has having 'more gable ends than a lazy man would care to count on a sunny day' together with 'huge zig-zag chimneys'. Later, he famously wrote to his friend and biographer, John Forster, "Chigwell, my dear fellow is the greatest place in the world; name your day of going to such a delicious old inn'.

At this time it was also a favourite venue for the officials of public authorities, who would enjoy banqueting here at the general expense.

During World War Two, the Kings Head was a favourite bolt hole for Winston Churchill. He would slip away from the cabinet war rooms, when time and events allowed, for a quiet evening meal in one of the upstairs rooms.

High Road, Chigwell, IG7 6QA

Date visited

Cap & Feathers, Tillingham

Once known as the Kings Head, this building, parts of which date back to 1420, was an alehouse by about 1600. It changed its name at the time of the civil war but no one seems to know where the new name originated from. At one time there was an undertakers business in the back of the premises, and one of the wooden archways has a piece carved out so that the undertaker could enter carrying a coffin without having to bend.

In 1792, the pub changed hands for £600. The new owner financed the cost of this by obtaining a fifteen year mortgage at an annual rate of 4 ½%.

Considering the age of the property, it's not surprising that there are at least two ghosts reputed to be on the premises. One is a former landlord and old sea-dog, by the name of Captain Cook, who has sometimes been heard playing tunes on beer bottles. It seems that, as well as a musician, he is also a real ale enthusiast and this explains why he has been known to go into the cellar and turn off the gas to the inferior keg beers.

Another ghost is that of a tall woman, who after the building had been disturbed during some renovations, was supposedly seen performing the favourite ghost trick of walking through walls.

Tillingham Hotspur Football Club was formed in 1903, and initially the players used the 'Feathers' as a changing room. Another link to that sport, although maybe of a higher standard, was during the 1970s when former England player, Neil Franklin, took over as landlord. He was once described by the legendary Sir Tom Finney as the best centre-half he had ever played with or against.

In 1949, the village of Tillingham was thrust into the national spotlight when the dismembered body of small-time crook, Stanley Setty, was found on the marshes. He had been missing for some time and a not-inconsiderate reward of £1,000 had been put up by his relatives. It was farm worker and Feather's dart-player, Syd Tiffin, who found the body whilst out duck shooting on the marshes. He then enjoyed his fifteen minutes of fame culminating with his photograph appearing in the Daily Mirror.

Despite his reward, which was the equivalent to him of four years pay, he still managed to find something to moan about. Apparently, at one time and another he had found nine other bodies on the marshes and each time the police had given him five shillings. He complained afterwards that they hadn't paid him on this occasion, and wanted to know why.

During the 1960s, there was a large and very lifelike, stuffed bear standing in the corner of the saloon bar, together with the knife that had reputedly killed the beast. It had been given to the pub by an old lady who lived on a nearby farm but history does not recall what eventually happened to it.

In 1987 the Feathers was purchased by the Crouch Vale Brewery and it then became their first tied pub. They have since relinquished ownership but it still receives regular CAMRA awards for the quality of its beer.

8-10 South Street, Tillingham, CM0 7TJ

Date visited

Black Horse, White Roding

Some time ago, a ghost at the Black Horse used to play, at night, weird and beautiful music on the pub piano. However, when the landlord quietly crept downstairs and opened the door the music would immediately stop. Walking into the deserted bar, he could see that the piano lid was firmly closed.

Eventually, the landlord got rid of the piano, but never-the-less the music was still occasionally heard. Once, when a couple were staying for bed and breakfast they asked the next morning who it was they had heard playing the piano during the night.

There have been other strange occurrences here. Doors have been known to be opened and closed by some invisible hand, and bottles and glasses left on the bar have been found later, moved to different positions. Legend says it's the work of the ghost of a cavalier who was brutally murdered nearby.

On one occasion two men followed an old man, hobbling with a walking stick, into the bar, but when they followed him in he was nowhere to be seen.

Chelmsford Road, White Roding, Dunmow, CM6 1RF

Date visited	

Chequers Inn, Goldhanger

The Chequers began life in the early 1400s as a courthouse. Those charged could be tried and sentenced here, executed outside in the square and then buried in the adjacent churchyard. Considering that the inn is only a few minutes walk from the River Blackwater, there is little doubt that some smugglers of the time would have suffered this fate.

The name originated from when the collector of taxes for the local church would visit here to collect money due from villagers who lived in its properties. He would use a board of black and white squares to help him whilst counting the money, and as each person made their payment he would place a coin on one square. When every square had been covered he knew his task had been completed.

In the early 1900s, Prince Nicholas of the Russian Imperial Court stayed here whilst in the country on a hunting trip.

Church Street, Goldhanger, Maldon, CM9 8AS

Date visited

Gardeners Arms, Loughton

It is quite a steep climb from Loughton High Road to the Gardeners Arms, hidden away at the top of York Hill, and anyone walking it too fast would probably need a whiff of oxygen before starting on the beer.

In fact this pub is one of the highest points in Essex and from the balcony at the back there are spectacular views over the county towards Canary Wharf, and onwards to the hills of Kent. Locals used to call this 'Wigan Pier' and during World War Two people would sit here and watch the night sky lighting up with the bombs and incendiaries being dropped during the blitz.

Originally a teahouse, this pub dates back to the 16th century, although various bits have been added to it since then. It now has a delightful charm that no modern architect could possibly reproduce. The small bar along the front opens up at the rear into a larger area with a high ceiling that creates a barn-like effect.

The high walls in this area are covered with a lot of interesting old pictures, as well as some other pieces of bric-a-brac. There's also a rack with a few rifles resting in it, although thankfully they're chained up just in case someone decided to get hold of one.

In a frame on one wall is the front page of the Morning Advertiser from the day it was first issued in February 1794. As well as national news, it includes articles about the latest performance at Covent Garden theatre, and an advertisement for the forthcoming English State Lottery.

There's also a nice photograph, from the turn of the last century, showing a horse and trap standing in front of the pub, along with some of the regulars of the time. The photo to the right which dates from 1899 may have been taken by the same person at the same time.

It would have been hard work for any horse that had to climb the hill whenever its owner fancied a quick pint, although it was probably even worse for the dray horses whenever they had to drag a wagon load of beer up there.

The only animals regularly seen here now are the various dogs who accompany their owners here, especially on a Sunday lunch-time. However, they all seem well behaved and are content to lounge around and have a quiet snooze, probably to get over the exertions of walking to the pub and in preparation for their return walk home.

103 York Hill, Loughton, IG10 1RX

Date visited	

Lobster Smack, Canvey Island

The Lobster Smack is one of the oldest buildings on Canvey Island, although no one seems really sure when it was actually constructed. Certainly there has been a pub on this site since at least 1563, although the general consensus is that this later building dates from the early 18th century.

During its lifetime it has been known by different names. These include The Sluice Inn, The Worlds End and The Lobster Pot. To the locals though it is just known as the Lobby.

A notice on the outside informs visitors that this was the Sluice House that featured in Charles Dickens' classic tale, Great Expectations. In the story Pip walked here through the rain-soaked marshes, only to be pounced upon and then tied up by the thoroughly unpleasant Mr. Orlick.

In 1879, Charles Dickens Junior, son of the famous novelist, published a book entitled Dictionary of the Thames from Oxford to the Nore. In this he commented that the Lobster Smack was 'comfortable and unobtrusive' and that 'boating men are frequently accommodated with good bed and board'.

Because of its isolated location, this pub was always a notorious haunt for smugglers, who could simply jump over the sea wall to unload contraband goods from the ships that were lying at anchor in nearby Hole Haven Creek. However, because a pub was an obvious place for the authorities to look for such goods, it was not unusual for them to be hidden in the nearby church, before being shipped inland later when the coast was clear.

The Lobster Smack would also regularly host bare knuckle fighting, a method often used to settle family feuds. One such grudge match took place on 22 September 1853, when Ben Court, aged 42, and 37 year-old Nat Langham fought no less than 60 rounds before deciding to shake hands, call the fight a draw and end their quarrel. During this bout Langham had been knocked down no less than 59 times.

In the case of weatherboarded houses there is always a great risk of fire, and this pub nearly succumbed when fire broke out one night back in 1933. Thankfully the men from nearby Benfleet fire station were able to get there in time, and although badly damaged the pub was rescued. The landlord at the time, James Went, praised the men's actions and told a local paper that the pub had been "saved for future generations of Essex folk to visit." How right he was.

Another landlord, from around 1845, is worth a mention although not for doing anything spectacular. He was in the Royal Navy at the time of Trafalgar, but managed to avoid the battle, and only merits a mention here because of his flamboyant name. This unfortunate chap went through life saddled with the name of Crisp Molyneux Harridge.

Coincidently, had he been around during World War Two he could have served his country and stayed at this pub at the same time. This is because in 1939 the pub became a 'stone frigate', the naval term for a shore-based establishment, and for a while during the conflict sailors from the Royal Navy were stationed on the upper floor.

Haven Road, Canvey Island, SS8 0NR

Date visited	

Rodney, Little Baddow

The Rodney was originally built as a farmhouse around the year 1650, and since then its early days are pretty much clouded in mystery. It is known that by the end of the 18th century it was owned by the family of Thomas Hodges, who in 1812 was co-founder of the Chelmsford Brewery Company.

It was first recorded as a pub in 1845, when Charles Smith was listed as a baker and beer retailer, although at the time it was then called the Dray. He also established a grocery shop on the premises.

To confuse matters, there was at this time another pub in the village called The Rodney. This had been named after Admiral George Rodney, who had a distinguished naval career culminating in a great victory over the French fleet in 1782.

When that pub closed in about 1867, the name and sign were transferred down the hill to this pub. The original pub then reopened for a while as The Rodney Pleasure Gardens, and for a while there were two establishments, very near to each other, bearing very similar names.

In 1900, the property, 'complete with a good garden and an enclosure of pasture land', was sold for £800. Previously it had been leased out by the brewery, presumably to ensure that the tenant bought only their own beers.

In 1902, to celebrate the coronation of Edward VII, the school children and all the parishioners of Little Baddow were entertained to tea at the Rodney. However a planned programme of sports was cancelled because the coronation was delayed by a couple of months due to the king's illness. The food would have spoiled so the organisers decided to go ahead with the tea.

There have been at least 4 ships in the Royal Navy named after Admiral Rodney, the last being a battleship that fought in World War Two. In 1941 it was part of a force which sank the German battleship Bismarck in the Atlantic after a chase lasting 4 days. Later on it took part in the Normandy landings. The badge of this ship now has pride of place on the outside wall of this pub.

After the end of the war, new tenants moved in here and began a series of improvements to the facilities. Until then, the landlord and his family shared a one bucket lavatory with the customers. Later a room behind the bar was converted into a private bar with a serving hatch to pass the beer through. Apparently there was a regular card school held here every Sunday morning.

Now the Rodney has been further extended and has a mainly maritime theme. There is an impressive collection of photographs, models and documents in addition to brasses and other naval bric-a-brac.

North Hill, Little Baddow, Chelmsford, CM 4TQ

Date visited

Saracen's Head, Dunmow

The original parts of the Saracen's Head are thought to be about 500 years old, although the Georgian frontage was only added in the 18th century. The name is an old one, dating back to the days of the crusaders, and it's possible that the present inn is the successor to an even earlier one which stood here in those times.

It has always been the most important inn in the town and has played a central part in its history. One of its early 17th century landlords, a chap by the name of Deane, was a man of affairs, and his son Sir Richard Deane became Lord Mayor of London in 1628. The Deanes were ardent supporters of Oliver Cromwell, and it's known that Cromwell himself stayed at the Saracen's Head on various occasions.

In the next century there was another famous landlord. He was thought by all to be a worthy and pious man, and always seemed considerate to the needs of his guests. However, this 'Jekyll and Hyde' led a double life and was by night a highwayman, often robbing his guests down country lanes after they had confided their fears and travel plans to him. Sometimes they would return to the inn, and he would sympathise with them whilst declaiming the villainy of robbery on the highway.

In 1864, a grand banquet and ball was held here on 24th February, to celebrate the coming of the railway. The first cut of this construction was made with a silver spade, and the 'Dunmow Flyer' served the community until 1952 when the line was closed.

The town of Dunmow is host every four years to 'The Flitch Trials' which are thought to date back to the start of the 1100s. This trial requires a married couple to stand before a mock court, and prove that they have for a year and a day 'not wished themselves unwed'. If they are able to do so to the satisfaction of the judge and jury, they are rewarded with a half side of salted pork which is known as a flitch.

Although most of the interior walls have now been removed, there were at one time many different rooms downstairs, and each was put to a different use. The bar to the left on entering the building used to be called the Commercial room and on market days it became the Corn Exchange. Another room at the back was the Smoke Room where generations of travellers sought rest and refreshment.

In the days when the Saracen's Head was a coaching inn, there were stables in the yard at the rear, and next to them was the ostler's tap room. It was here that coachmen and grooms, awaiting their master's pleasure, passed the time in gossip of the road, with a tankard or two of beer that had been brewed on the premises.

High Street, Great Dunmow, CM6 1AG

Date visited	

Ye Olde Albion, Rowhedge

Around the year 1750, a ruthless gang of smugglers used the Albion as a meeting place to discuss their illicit operations. They did this openly and with no fear of capture, because they had bribed the local Customs officer. However, one night the greedy official demanded an increased share of the spoils, and when the smugglers refused he foolishly threatened to report them to the authorities.

At the time, smuggling was a hanging offence and the desperate gang decided that their best plan of action was to silence the officer once and for all. A rope was brought in and the unfortunate man was hanged, there and then, from a hook fixed in the bar ceiling. To this day the hook still remains, embedded in one of the overhead beams.

Locals say that the ghost of this unfortunate chap now haunts the pub, and he has been seen both inside and outside the pub, still dressed in his red-jacketed uniform.

High Street, Rowhedge, Colchester, CO5 7ES

| Date visited | |

White Hart, Margaretting Tye

The White Hart is a traditional Essex weather-boarded building. It started life as a couple of cottages about 250 years ago, and is sited on a green known locally as Tigers Island. The 'Island' derived from the fact that when the nearby River Wid flooded, and the waters rose, it never quite reached as high as the pub.

'Tigers' was the Victorian name given to the labourers working on the nearby railway. They would congregate here after work, and often the evening would end with them outside, engaged in bare-knuckle fights to settle the disputes which inevitably arose.

Now things are more genteel, and every summer a large marquee is erected in the garden to house the ever popular beer festival. This usually occurs at the end of June and consists of five nights of live music, at least 60 real ales and a convivial atmosphere. Not to be missed.

Swan Lane, Margaretting Tye, CM4 9JX

Date visited

St Annes Castle, Great Leighs

St Annes Castle claims to be the oldest pub in the country and a notice on the wall states that it was mentioned in the Domesday Book of 1086. At one time it was a hermitage, and following the murder of Thomas a Becket, it was used as a stop-over for pilgrims on their way to visit the martyr's shrine in Canterbury.

The rather undistinguished exterior of this tavern is the result of a major fire, during the mid 1800s, which destroyed a large part of the inn. However, it was rebuilt around the shell of the original building and inside many of the early timbers still remain. At the same time the original thatched roof was replaced with one of tiles.

There are many ghostly stories associated with this pub including that of a former landlady who refused to enter one of the bedrooms because of the evil presence she felt there. Apparently, her Alsatian dog was also uncomfortable in this room and if dragged in there, its hair would rise on its neck and the dog would whine to be let out.

One story is that a child was murdered in that room long ago, but it's so distant now that no details remain of what actually happened.

Another ghost that haunts the 'Castle' is thought to be that of a witch who was burned at the stake in the village during the Middle Ages. She was buried with a stake through her heart at the nearby Scrap Faggot Green crossroads and a large boulder placed over her grave to prevent her evil spirit from escaping. However during the Second World War, there were a lot of large American military trucks in the area, and as they couldn't negotiate their vehicles around the boulder they sent the bulldozers in to remove it.

From that time some quite peculiar things began to happen. This included the switching of scores of ducks and hens between neighbouring farms in the middle of one night. This would have been a very noisy operation, but surprisingly not a sound was heard. Nobody knows if this was a supernatural joke played by the witch, but certainly the moving of livestock in this manner was a practice that Essex witches were often accused of.

There is also the story of a drayman from the Romford Brewery Company, who was delivering beer into the cellar and claimed to have come face to face with a ghost. He ran back to his dray and was found there ashen-faced and shaking. He vowed never to go into that cellar again and from then on was transferred to another round.

However in 1996, after a team of psychic investigators visited the pub and carried out a thorough investigation, they failed to detect any signs of paranormal activity. So perhaps, at last, the ghosts have gone.

Main Road, Great Leighs, CM3 1NE

Date visited

Index of Pubs

138

Lamarsh, *Lamarsh Lion* 114
Langley Lower Green, *Bull* 48
Leigh-on-Sea, *Crooked Billet* 66
Little Baddow, *Rodney* 130
Little Totham, *Swan* 70
Lobster Smack, Canvey Island 128
Loughton, *Gardeners Arms* 126
Maldon, *Swan* 15
Manningtree, *White Hart* 62
Margaretting Tye, *White Hart* 135
Marquis, Colchester 92
Mitre, Wickham Bishops 105
Mole Hill Green, *Three Horseshoes* 40
Moreton, *Nags Head* 56
Mountnessing, *George & Dragon* 14
Nags Head, Moreton 56
North Fambridge, *Ferry Boat Inn* 115
North Weald, *Kings Head* 110
Paglesham, *Plough & Sail* 38
Paul Pry, Rayleigh 90
Pebmarsh, *Kings Head* 84
Peldon Rose, Peldon 86
Peldon, *Peldon Rose* 86
Plough & Sail, Paglesham 38
Queens Head, Great Clacton 6
Rainbow and Dove, Hastingwood 55
Rayleigh Arms, Terling 85
Rayleigh, *Paul Pry* 90
Red Lion, Billericay 108
Red Lion, Kirby-le-Soken 116
Rochford, *Kings Head* 104
Rodney, Little Baddow 130
Rose & Crown, Ashdon 74
Rose & Crown, Writtle 68
Rowhedge, *Ye Olde Albion* 134
Roxwell, *Chequers* 100
Saffron Walden, *Cross Keys* 58
Saracens Head, Great Dunmow 132
Shalford, *George* 96
Shoulder of Mutton, Fordham 34
Sible Hedingham, *White Horse* 24

South Benfleet, *Anchor* 26
St Annes Castle, Great Leighs 136
Stanford Rivers, *Woodman* 60
Star, Ingatestone 98
Stock, *Cock* 12
Sun Hotel, Dedham 112
Sun, Feering 20
Swan, Braintree 8
Swan, Brentwood 64
Swan, Little Totham 70
Swan, Maldon 15
Swan, Thaxted 22
Terling, *Rayleigh Arms* 85
Thatchers, Hatfield Heath 95
Thaxted, *Swan* 22
Three Horseshoes, Mole Hill Green 40
Tillingham, *Cap and Feathers* 122
Tolleshunt Major, *Bell* 94
Travellers Friend, Woodford Green 25
Wendens Ambo, *Bell* 28
Whalebone, Fingringhoe 52
White Hart Inn, Halstead 30
White Hart, Manningtree 62
White Hart, Margaretting Tye 135
White Hart, Witham 82
White Horse, Sible Hedingham 24
White Lion, Fobbing 16
White Roding, *Black Horse* 124
Wickham Bishops, *Mitre* 105
Witham, *White Hart* 82
Wivenhoe, *Black Buoy* 78
Wooden Fender, Ardleigh 45
Woodford Green, *Travellers Friend* 25
Woodham Walter, *Bell* 36
Woodman, Stanford Rivers 60
Woolpack, Coggeshall 88
Wormingford, *Crown* 54
Writtle, *Rose & Crown* 68
Ye Olde Albion, Rowhedge 134
Ye Olde Kings Head, Chigwell 120
Yew Tree, Great Horkesley 32

Bibliography

A Discovery of Old Essex	Richard Pusey
A Garland of Hops	James Wentworth Day
A History of Witham	Janet Gyford
Another Miller's Tale	Geoff Austin
Around Danbury and Little Baddow	Jill Goodson
Barking Pubs Past and Present	Tony Clifford
Best Inns and Pubs	James Lawrence
Billericay and its High Street	Harry Richman
Colne Engaine, Reflections of Our Village	Jill Fleming
Essex Countryside Magazine	Various Articles
Essex Rich and Strange	Richard Pusey
Famous Smugglers Inns	Frank Graham
Forever Young's	Helen Osbourne
Give Them Enough Ale	Michael Bardell
Haunted Pubs in Britain and Ireland	Marc Alexander
Here's Good Luck to the Pint Pot	Kevin Brown
Historic English Inns	Ted Bruning & Keith Paul
Horndon on the Hill, Ancient & Modern	Winifred M Tinworth
Ingatestone and Fryerning	Ian Yearsley
Inns & Taverns of Colchester	Jess A Jephcott
Kelvedon and its Antiquities	B L Kentish
Mole Hill Green History	Pat Salmon
Old Inns and Alehouses of Epping	Chris Johnson
Pubs of Essex	R M Smith
Rayleigh, Its People and Places	Ernest H Lane
Rochford, A History	Mavis Sipple
Roxwell Revealed	Roxwell Revealed Group
Stock	Charles Phillips
The English Country Inn	Gary Hogg
The English Inn	Thomas Burke
The Essex Village Book	Essex Women's Institute
The Haunted Pub Guide	Guy Lyon Playfair
The Inns of Billericay	Grant Wyn
The Romance of Essex Inns	Glyn H Morgan
The Taverns of Old England	H P Maskell
Timpson's English Country Inns	John Timpson
Wivenhoe Pubs	Peter Kay
Writtle Inns	Sue Bell